UTTER DISASTER
ON THE OREGON TRAIL

Snake Country Series
(forthcoming)

Volume I
The Boise Massacre
Attack on the Ward Party in 1854 and Massacres of 1859

Volume III
Massacre Rocks and City of Rocks
1862 Attacks on Emigrant Trains

The

Utter Disaster

On The Oregon Trail

The Utter and Van Ornum Massacres of 1860

by

Donald H. Shannon

Volume II
Snake Country Series

Cover design by Kathleen Petersen

Snake Country Publishing
Caldwell, Idaho
1993

Library of Congress Catalog Card Number: 93-83498

ISBN   0-9635828-2-8

Project managed and distributed by
Tamarack Books
P O Box 190313
Boise, ID 83719-0313
1-800-962-6657 or 208-362-1543

Printed in the United States of America

To Janet

Emeline Trimble Fuller
As pictured in her 1892 book.

Contents

Illustrations

Figures

Maps

Foreword

Westward bound emigrants usually began their journey with preconceived fears regarding the possibility of an unfriendly encounter with the various Indian tribes situated along the route. Somewhat ironically, once they passed Independence Rock many considered the threat to be over. However, they soon learned that the chances of an Indian attack increased dramatically as they passed over the Bear River Divide and entered the Snake River Plain and the California Trail corridor.

Until the 1854 Ward disaster, emigrants enjoyed a relatively peaceful relationship with the Native Americans encountered along the Snake River routes. Isolated incidents did occur, but the relationship tended to be more amicable than confrontational. The situation began to change in the 1850's after the Hudson Bay Company abandoned their Snake River posts, and the native inhabitants became increasingly alarmed at the number of emigrants traversing through their homelands. During this time, hostile encounters increased and emigrants began to clamor for protection.

When news of the Utter disaster reached populated western settlements, the outcry for better protection increased substantially. Their sufferings reinforced the need to establish military posts along the various routes, and the desire to punish all the guilty parties.

The plight of the survivors has attracted attention for many years. The inhuman suffering, the number of casualties and the tactics of the attack greatly added to the fears of those who followed. The casualty count was the highest of any recorded along the trail, and the tactics employed proved to be unique. Generally, attacks on emigrant trains were hit and run, but in this incident, a prolonged attack was sustained against the encircled wagon train for two days. Survivors also related the appearance of white men among the perpetrators which amplified the anxiety of those who followed.

Until recently, all versions identified the train as the Otter
party. Contemporary accounts can be held responsible for the
misspelling. The name is of German derivation and when
pronounced sounds like Otter. The correct spelling was uncovered during the research for this book. Early reports were
also confused as to the location of the encounter. All agreed it
occurred somewhere below Salmon Falls, but that is where the
consensus ended. Survivors were unable to adequately identify the site, and that added to the confusion.

This work is the culmination of many years of research
and successfully addresses the many inaccuracies and questions surrounding the tragic events associated with the disaster.
The documentation factually relates the story as it unfolded and
enables the reader to better comprehend this compelling story.

LARRY R. JONES
Idaho Historical Society Historian

Preface

MASSACRE! The word is harsh and often misleading when applied to Indian attacks on emigrant wagon trains on the Oregon and California Trails of the last century. It literally means "the act or an instance of killing a number of usually helpless or unresisting human beings under circumstances of atrocity or cruelty."* Of the two greatest tragedies, which occurred in the Snake River Country, the term is aptly applied to the Ward Massacre of 1854, and the Utter Disaster and Van Ornum Massacres of 1860.

These sad events continually interest people. Newspapers still print articles on the subject—based on outdated, inaccurate, and incomplete accounts. Miles Cannon's stirring stories of the Otter (Utter) Massacre still make exciting reading. Cannon's research (about the time of World War I) though, erroneously placed the site of the Indian attack at Sinker Creek instead of further east toward Castle Butte (both sites are just south of the Snake River in Owyhee County, Idaho). Annie Laurie Bird's history, *Boise, The Peace Valley* (published in 1934), contained an excellent account of the Ward Massacre, based on data then available. Much information has come to light in the ensuing years, and has created a need for a definitive, comprehensive, and more accurate rendition of these happenings. Nor is there a detailed and orderly accounting of the 1862 encounters at Massacre Rocks, those at City of Rocks, and the 1859 attacks. This book is confined to giving a detailed account of the Utter and Van Ornum massacres of 1860 and subsequent attempts to rescue the captive children. This volume, with its forthcoming prequel—*The Boise Massacre* (recounting the attack on the Ward party in 1854 and

---

Webster's New Collegiate Dictionary, 1974.

the massacres of 1859)— and sequel—*Massacre Rocks and City of Rocks* (the 1862 attacks on emigrant trains)—form the trilogy of the Snake Country Massacres series.

The major sources of information for the *Utter Disaster* come from four accounts or interviews given by Joseph Myers[M] in November 1860, the 1892 book of Emeline Trimble Fuller,[E] the 8 November 1860 Army report of Captain Frederick T. Dent,[D] the 1927 private manuscript of Margaret Myers Beers,[MM] and a 1922 interview of Isabella Myers Martin.[IM] The following historical narrative is more in the form of a 'chronicle' so as to include portions of the often well-written and gripping accounts by survivors and witnesses of these disastrous encounters. Thus, the readers can draw their own conclusions and interpretations from these events. The quotes within this volume are faithful to the original forms, including spelling and punctuation. As noted above, the sources are mainly cited in the text by a letter in superscript, instead of being referenced with an Arabic numeral.

Acknowledgments

Over eight years of research have taken me to the historical societies, university and state libraries in six western states, as well as the National Archives and the Library of Congress. I wish to thank Colonel (Ret.) Gerald Evans of Stockton, CA, a descendant of Margaret Myers Beer, for permission to use her manuscript. Mr. Frank L. Tyler of Nampa, ID, a descendant of the Myers, also furnished some information. Foremost, though, I wish to acknowledge the contribution and assistance provided by Larry Jones of the Idaho Historical Society who over the years had gathered much of the material and became an authoritative source on the Snake Country massacres. Also thanks to the staff of the Idaho Historical Society Library— Guila Ford, Elizabeth Jacox, and John Yandell—and staff of the Idaho Historical Society Genealogical Library.

Gordon Manning, Margaret Haines, and Todd Shafer were quite helpful during several visits to the Oregon Historical Society, as were Elaine Miller and Joy Werlink at the Washington State Historical Society while doing research there. I wish to thank Ann McMurrin of the Utah State Historical Society; Phillip I. Earl, Nevada Historical Society; Terry Abraham, University of Idaho, Special Collections and Archives; Nan Cohen and staff, University of Washington Libraries, Special Collections, Manuscripts and Archives; Jeanne Engerman and Gail, Washington State Library at Olympia; and staffs of the National Archives in the Microfilm Reading Room, Old Army Records, Cartographic Center, and Central Reading Room. Thanks also to the staffs of the LDS Genealogical Library; the Golden Room of the California State Library; the Idaho State Law Library; and to Dale Gray, Julie Hyslop, and Linda of the Owyhee County Historical Society; Robert Hamilton of the Canyon County Historical Society; to Jason Nettleton for permission to explore Castle Butte; Cathy Cross and Eric Shannon for an early reviewing of the manuscript; Jim Oates for his enthusiastic interest in the research; and for Janet Shannon's aid in the final editing.

Special thanks to the Idaho Historical Society, Idaho Bicentennial Commission, and Idaho Transportation Department for the courtesy of the drawings at the end of chapters and page 190.

Left by the Indians.

Story of My Life.

EMELINE L. FULLER.

Snake Country Massacres

1854

19 August   Attack on a train on Goodale Cutoff in Camas Prairie (Camas or Elmore County, Idaho)

20 August   **Ward Massacre** along Boise River (south of Middleton, Canyon County, Idaho)

1859

26 July   Small emigrant train attacked at Cold Springs in the Bear River area (either on the Hudspeth Cutoff in Idaho or Sublette Cutoff in Wyoming).

27 July   **Shepherd Massacre** in the Bear River area (either on the Hudspeth Cutoff in Idaho or Sublette Cutoff in Wyoming).

12-13 August   Dragoon force fight Shoshoni in Box Elder canyon (between Cache Valley and Brigham City, Utah)

20 August   Ambush of the Carpenter Train on Kinney's Cutoff (near juncture of Idaho, Wyoming, Utah borders)

31 August   **Miltimore Massacre** in the vicinity of the American Falls (Power County, Idaho)

1860

23 June   Attack on Army Wagon Road Party between Malheur and Owyhee rivers (Malheur County, Oregon)

c26 August   Sheep Train Attacked at Castle Butte (Owyhee County, Idaho)

7-9 September   Wagon Train Attacked within five miles of City of Rocks (Cassia County, Idaho)

9-10 September   **Utter Massacre** along Snake River, west of Castle Butte (Owyhee County, Idaho)

c23 September   Two Ex-Dragoons from Utter Train killed on headwaters of John Day River (Grant County, Oregon)

c16-18 October   **Van Ornum Massacre** at Farewell Bend (Huntington, Baker County, Oregon)

1861
8 August   Stock taken from Harriman Train at City of Rocks

1862
9 August   Attack on the Iowa City 'Salmon River Party' Train and then the Adams Train east of **Massacre Rocks** (Power County, Idaho)

10 August   Attack on the Indians by members from several wagon trains near Massacre Rocks (Power County, Idaho)

15 August   Attack on Wagon Trains near City of Rocks (Cassia County, Idaho)

20 August   Bristol-Kennedy train skirmishes with Indians on Rock Creek (Twin Falls County, Idaho)

12 September   Eastbound Californians attacked by Shoshoni in a running fight on Salt Lake City road along Raft River, east of City of Rocks

1863
29 January   **Bear River Massacre**: California Volunteers attack Shoshoni on Battle Creek (Franklin County, Idaho)

THE NEWS.

The event of which we have been in constant apprehension—and of which we have implored the proper authorities to guard against, has occurred—the murder of forty-five emigrants, bound for Oregon, 175 miles above the Dalles, on Salmon river. Who these emigrants are, we have no knowledge. They were undoubtedly emigrants who designed to make this valley their home—husbands, wives, children—coming here under the promised protection of government.   Horrible! horrible!

Oregonian, 6 October 1860

INTRODUCTION

The greatest disaster to befall an emigrant party on the Oregon Trail occurred in 1860, on the South Alternate Route in the Snake River Country of present day Idaho and Oregon. The Utter wagon train was attacked on the trail along the south side of the Snake River, just west of Castle Creek. This massacre site lies midway between Murphy and Grand View, Idaho; the Van Ornum Massacre occurred at Huntington, Oregon. The attack on the wagon train and subsequent attacks on the survivors resulted in the greatest loss of life to an emigrant train and to the attacking Indians, of any such encounters on the Oregon or California Trails.

The Indians of the Snake Country and the American West did not lack personal courage and did not fear to die, but they were not foolhardy and never attacked emigrants unless there was a chance of a favorable outcome. There were few occasions when Indians attacked a wagon train encircled for defense. In the massacres of 1859 and 1860, there is ample evidence that "renegade" white men were the instigators and even participants in almost all of these attacks. The Utter massacre was a rare instance when Indians not only attempted but maintained a protracted and successful attack on encircled emigrant wagons.

LIBBIE.   EMELINE.   CHRISTY.

Trimble Children
As pictured in Emeline L. Trimble Fuller's 1892 book, *Left by the Indians*

ONE

Families of the Utter Train

Most of the emigrants in the last wagon train crossing the Snake River plains for Oregon in 1860 came from southern Wisconsin, the others from neighboring states. The train consisted of eight ox teams and wagons, other animals, and four families with a number of single men. The Utter family was the largest in the wagon train. Three of this family's ten children were from Mrs. Abagel Payne Trimble Utter's former marriage. Elijah P. Utter had six children with him from his first marriage. The tenth child was born to Abagel and Elijah the previous fall.[1]

Abagel Payne bore three children in her first marriage, to Trimble. Emeline L. was born 21 February 1847 at Mercellon, Columbia County, Wisconsin. Emeline Trimble later wrote of their experiences in a book published in 1892: "Christopher was born Nov. 28th, 1850. He was always vigorous and full of fun." Elizabeth, or Libbie, "was born Jan. 9th, 1852. She was always a delicate child, and hence a great care to me." Abagel's son carried the name of her father, Christopher Payne.* Emeline related a couple of incidents that affected her physically. In 1852, when she was five, the Trimble family left Wisconsin and

> moved to Keokuk Co., Iowa. We traveled with oxen and wagon. When all was in readiness to start as we supposed, father noticed that he had not fixed a place to carry a pail with which to water the oxen on the

---

*See Appendix I, "The Paynes and the Trimbles," for Abagel's family history.

3

way. He took a nail and while driving it in a cross-piece under the wagon, the nail flew and struck my right eye as I was looking on, causing almost total loss of vision ever since. We arrived at Uncle William Trimble's after a journey of over two weeks. Father rented a house for us, and went to work at whatever he could get to do. In the fall of 1852 father, being away with a threshing machine, was called home on account of mother's sickness. She had the Typhoid fever. Soon after she recovered father took the same disease and died.

George Trimble, Emeline's Uncle, went to Iowa and moved Abagel and the three children back to Wisconsin and Walworth County. The other accident that caused a physical defect to Emeline?

Here I wish to mention a little incident that occurred, because of what follows. I loved my little brother Christy dearly. One day mother hid the axe from him for fear he might cut himself, but I found it and gave it to him. Soon after I was passing where he was chopping and accidently fell, and my left hand went under the axe as it came down and I lost my large finger for finding the axe. Children do suffer for not minding their parents. But poor Christy felt worse about it than I did. He cried as though his heart would break, and we could not get him to come in the house till late that night.

In the next six years the widowed Abagel and her three children remained in Wisconsin. They lived in six different homes with relatives. They stayed a year with Abagel's brother, George. In the spring of 1854 Abagel took her family to her parents' home in Winnebago County. That fall they went to Abagel's brother, Uriah Payne, who was a widower with three children. Abagel kept house for him until the following spring when she moved her family to Fond du Lac

County, near Brandon. They remained there about a year and a half, and then moved back to Columbia County to the home of yet another of Abagel's brothers, Jason Payne. The spring of 1857, a Trimble relative took the family back to Walworth County where Abagel helped to care for her deceased husband's parents.

Emeline Trimble described the conjoining of her family with that of the Utters. In May of 1858

> mother married Elijah Utter of Walworth Co., a black-smith by occupation, and a large-hearted honest man, who proved a good husband to mother, and a good father to us children. He had three sons and three daughters, making in all eleven in the family. The next year a baby daughter was born to them making twelve in the family.

Elijah Utter's six children from his first marriage were twenty-three-year-old Mary; teenage son, Charles; Henry, age twelve; Wesley, a boy of five years; and two small daughters, Emma and Abby. Susan was the infant born to Elijah and Abagel in September 1859.[2]

Throughout her book Emeline spelled the family name as *Utter*. This too was the spelling on Abagail and Elijah's marriage record.[3] (Emeline spelled her mother's name as *Abagel*). In their accounts, Joseph Myers and his daughter, Isabella, also spelled the name as *Utter*, but others who reported upon the Utter Disaster spelled the name *Otter*. The German pronunciation of *Utter* is quite similar to the way Americans pronounce *otter*. Emeline's stepfather and

> mother often talked of going to the far west to make themselves a home, and settle their numerous family in homes adjoining their own in that broad country, where settlers were so much needed to till the lands, and improve the country, and after much deliberation and very much advice from friends and neighbors, they decided to go and commenced preparations

forthwith, selling their home and converting other property into money, buying oxen and wagons, and preparing for our long journey, for we had decided that we would go to Oregon, which was a full six months journey in our way of travel.

In the latter part of 1859, all of the Utters joined with the Myers and Prime families in forming a company to start in the spring for Oregon and California.[4]

] The Myers Family [

The Joseph Myers family was also from Walworth County. They lived eight miles west of Geneva, near the lake. Five years before they had lived in Smelser Town, Grant County, Wisconsin. The family included Mary E. Prime Myers, Joseph (a farmer), and their five children. Isabella, the eldest of the four girls, was just under ten in this spring of 1860. The second daughter, Margaret, was seven. Eugene, the middle child, was five. The little lame girl, Harriet (called Hattie), was three. The infant, Carrie, was born the previous October.

Also traveling to Oregon was John W. Myers. John's home was likewise in the Lake Geneva area of Walworth County, just north of Hebron, Illinois. He was leaving behind his wife and eight children while he went ahead to find a new home. Joseph and John were to join their brother, a Mr. Michael Myers, who owned a grocery store in Salem. Emigrating also was Edwin Prime, the brother of Mary Myers. The Myers and Prime adults were born in upstate New York; the Myers children were born in Wisconsin.[5]

Two of the Myers' daughters also later wrote of their experiences. Isabella thought her father was born in New York state and her mother in Illinois. But Margaret differed:

My parents were both born in the State of New York, Father in Utica or Rochester, am uncertain as to which. Mother was born in Syracuse. Mother's parents, whose name was Prime, emigrated to Wisconsin when Mother was eleven years old. Father also went to Wisconsin when but eighteen, but whether with his parents or alone I do not know. If alone, his family soon followed. My parents were unknown to each other until Mother was grown, when they became acquainted and married, and made their home in Wisconsin for twelve years, when Father was seized with the desire to go to Oregon, a brother of his having gone out in 1853 and written glowing accounts of the country. A brother of my Mother's had also gone out to California in 1850 and returned to his home in Wisconsin but wanted to return to California.

So, in the fall and winter of '59 a company was formed to start in the spring of '60. As I was such a small girl I do not know how many started from the old home. However, on the first day of May, 1860, the long hazardous journey was begun. Our family consisted of my parents and five small children, the oldest past nine, the youngest just six months old, my father's brother and a woman of 25 or 26* who was to help mother with the children and camp work for her board and passage to Oregon.

Emeline Trimble described the beginning of their journey. As the first of May dawned upon them clear and bright:

with all prepared for starting, we yoked our oxen to the wagons, gathered our cows and young stock together, taking sixteen head and four yoke of oxen, our family dog, clothing, provisions, household utensils, etc. Although tears were in our eyes at the thought of parting with our friends and relatives, still we were hopeful, for we dearly loved each other, stepfather, stepbrothers and sisters all being united and happy, and the thought that in that far land to which we were

---

*This woman might have been Mary Utter.

to go, we would be so fortunate as to live an unbroken
family in nice homes, near father and mother, and if
the Lord will it, with not a face missing in our family
circle, gave strength to pass through the sorrowful
parting. But I shall never forget the tearful faces of
my dear old grandparents as they stood at the end of
the lane, leading to the road, with tears streaming
down their wrinkled faces, bid a last adieu to their
youngest child and her family.

I was then a girl of 13 years, and with a heart un-
touched by cares, but bitterly did I cry over leaving
home, and lonely, most lonely were the first few
nights of camping, and feeling that we were going farther and farther from home each day.

We fell in with three other teams about noon of the
first day, that like ourselves were started for Oregon
and California. . . . With this addition to our company
we felt stronger and better satisfied.

The Myers, with two wagons, joined the Utters on the first
day of travel and were with them the entire journey. The other
wagon of these Walworth County neighbors was Prime's.

Being well outfitted, we had all the comforts one
could have travelling with oxen over those seemingly
endless miles, sometimes camping where water and
grass were plentiful and sometimes making what they
know as a "dry camp." To provide for such an emergency, they carried a large barrel fitted in a frame on
the back of one wagon. Many started with one wagon
and four oxen. My [Margaret's] father had two stout
wagons and six yoke or twelve oxen, and drove his
two fresh milch cows. A brother (Uncle John) drove
one team, my father the other.[MM]

The emigrant families soon became used to traveling on the
trail and accustomed to camp life. After awhile some actually
enjoyed it.

Everything had been planned before starting on our journey, and we had prepared all things for convenience on the road. We took ten milch cows, and had kegs made before starting, and we milked our cows and strained the milk into kegs, put them into our wagons, and every night the milk was churned by the motion of the wagons into nice butter, which we salted and worked into balls for us.

We stopped and rested our teams occasionally, and did our washings and such work as it was possible to do up ahead under the circumstances.[E]

The emigrants traveled west to the Mississippi River. There nine-year-old Isabella Myers met her future husband for the first time

at Galena, Ill., where U. S. Grant was then living. That was in the spring of 1860. We were passing through in our prairie schooners on our way to Oregon. Will [Martin] was a clerk in a store, and he brought out a bag of candy for us children.

The Utter group passed through Iowa to Council Bluffs and crossed the Missouri River at Omaha. They left there 5 June and followed the Platte River Road. This route was still being used by the Mormons in their annual migration. Merrill J. Mattes wrote in *The Great Platte River Road* that "those who started in the Council Bluffs-Omaha area, being on the north side of the Platte, were apt to stay there until they came to Fort Laramie."[6] The month passed with many things of interest occurring. The men took part in a buffalo hunt. Owing to the fact that Margaret Myers' Uncle Michael

had crossed seven years previous without being molested by Indians, they expected no trouble with them. However, my mother was always fearful and seemed to have a forewarning of trouble. When the others of the company were happy and carefree she was anxious and depressed. When we got into the Indian country she was watchful of every sign.[MM]

The Utter and Myers party kept falling in with other emigrant teams travelling along the Platte. By the time they reached Fort Laramie they were in quite a train of wagons. "Ox hooves wore down to the quick, usually by the time Fort Laramie was reached, and this required attention."[7] So the emigrants stopped at Fort Laramie a few days to rest and to have the ox teams reshod. They were waiting for other emigrants which they heard were behind them on the trail and also bound for Oregon. As they continued traveling, some congratulated themselves on now being so far on their journey that they were out of danger from the Indians. Emeline Trimble wrote:

> We fell in with a large California train, and traveled with them until the Californian trail separated from Oregon . . . While with the Californian train, when we camped at night we would prepare the ground, and have a good old fashioned dance. It was not much work to make our toilets, for most of us wore for convenience the costume called Bloomers and did not have many changes. We would also sing songs, tell stories, and amuse ourselves with all the sports of our school days, feeling perfectly safe and secure, for in union was our strength.

The emigrants had finished crossing the Nebraska Territory and were at the Continental Divide, at South Pass. They probably separated from the larger California train here, as this was where the more northern Lander Road branched off from the main route to Oregon. The Lander Road was completed the year before and cut off some sixty to seventy miles from the older route of the Oregon Trail.[8] Some four to seven days less travel time would make a difference to the emigrants. But then, the Oregon-bound emigrants may have followed the older Sublette Cutoff, remaining with the California train as far as Soda Springs. There the larger train would take Hudspeth's

Cutoff to meet the California Trail on the Raft River. Somewhere along the way the Utter party had an antelope hunt and
attempted to shoot a Rocky Mountain sheep.

] The Van Ornum Party and the Chases [

Those teams bound for Oregon under the leadership of
Elijah Utter now totaled eight wagons. Of the other teams
headed for Oregon, three wagons belonged to the Van Ornums
and one to the Chase family. The Chases were from Geneva,
Kane County, Illinois. Daniel and Elizabeth Chase had boys
eight and six years old and a girl age two. The *Kane County
Directory* (1859) listed a Mr. Daniel A. Chase as a tinsmith in
Geneva, Illinois whose house was on the corner of Hamilton
and Third. As there seems to be no other record of the Chase
family in Geneva, Illinois, their residence there must have been
transitory. Mrs. Chase had a brother, John Pierce, living in
Washington Territory on Puget Sound.[9]

There were thirteen in the Van Ornum Party. Alexis and
Abigail Van Ornum had five children ranging in age from sixteen to six. They were from Wiota Town, Lafayette County,
Wisconsin. Alexis was taking his family to join his younger
brother, Zacheus, who had gone overland to Oregon in 1851.[10]

Zacheus Van Ornum had been born at Ellery, Chautauqua
County, New York, 16 April 1828. "My grand Father was a
Prisnor 8 years in the Revolution 1776 and my Father Served
under Scott in 1812." Later, at age seventy-five, in an Oregon
Pension application he would also attest, "That my full name is
Zacheus VanOrnum* and the spelling thereto correct."[11]

Van Ornum was the way Zacheus consistently spelled his name in all correspondence from 1896 to
1903 regarding his pension application. *Vanornum* was the spelling used for Alexis in the 1850 Federal Census
and the *1855 Wisconsin State Census*; the Christian name was spelled *Alexus* in the former. *Van Orman* and
Vanorman was the spelling for Zacheus' family and his relatives in the 1870 Census. The latter spelling was
also used in the 1880 Census and in Captain Dent's 1860 Army report. Emeline Trimble spelled the name *Van
Orman*. So too did Margaret Myers. *Vannorman, Van Norman, Manorman, McNorman,* and *Vernorman* are other
spellings encountered in reports and writings on the Van Ornums. The Oregon Historical Society spells the
name *Vanorum* in its Pioneer File Index, but *Van Ornum* in the Biography Index. A granddaughter referred to
Zacheus (or Zachias) as *Grandpa Van Ornum*. (See Endnote 12.)

Utter family: (Otter) from Walworth Co., Wisconsin   **12**
Elijah P. Utter
Abagel Payne Trimble Utter,   b. 12 Jul 1827, Galena WI
Mary Utter   about 23
Emeline L. Trimble   13, b. 21 Feb 1847 Mercellon WI
Charles Utter, 'Charlie'   12 or 13, a lad
Henry Utter   11 or 12 years
Christopher Trimble, 'Christy,' 10, b. 28 Nov 1850 WI
Elizabeth Trimble, 'Libbie'   9, b. 9 Jan 1852 WI
Wesley Utter   5
Emma Utter   little girl (older than Abby)
Abby Utter   little girl
Susan Utter   born 10 Sep 1859 Walworth Co., WI

Myers: [Lake] Geneva, Walworth Co., Wisconsin   **8**
Joseph Myers   born Utica or Rochester NY
Mary E. Prime Myers   28, b. 14 Jul 1832 Syracuse NY
Isabella Myers   almost 10, born 13 Oct 1850 WI
Margaret Myers, 'Maggie'   7, born WI
Eugene Myers   5, born Oct 1854 WI
Harriet Myers, 'Hattie' (lame)   3, born WI
Carolyn Myers, 'Carrie'   1, born Oct 1859 WI
John W. Myers (brother to Joseph)

Chase family: from Geneva, Kane Co., Illinois   **5**
Daniel A. Chase, Sr.
Elizabeth Pierce Chase
Daniel Chase, Jr.   8
Albert Chase   6
Mary Chase   2

Members of the Utter Train.   (Compiled by Author).

Van Ornum (Van Orman) Party

Van Ornum family: Wiota Town, Lafayette Co., WI   7
Alexis Van Ornum (Alexus)   39, born NY
Abigail Van Ornum   39, born OH c1821
Marcus M. Van Ornum, 'Mark'   16 or 17, b. WI
Eliza Van Ornum   13, born WI
Minerva Van Ornum   11
Reuben Van Ornum   8
Lucinda Van Ornum   6

Boarding with the Van Ornums: 6
Judson Cressey
Samuel Gleason   young man
Lewis Lawson   from IA
Goodsel Munson   old gentleman
Reith brothers: Germans from Minnesota
    Jacob Reith, 'Jake'   early 20s, b. Alsace, France
    Joseph Reith, 'Joe'

Ex-Dragoons

Discharged Soldiers: 5
Sgt Charles Schamberg   27, Hess Cassell, Germany
Pvt Theodore Murdock   24, Baltimore MD
Pvt Henry Snyder   29, Lenning, Germany
Pvt Charles Kishnell   German
Pvt William Utley

Deserter: 1
Lucius (Charles) M. Chaffee   18, born Parker, [PA?]

Total members, day of attack: 44

Members of the Utter Train (Cont.).   (Compiled by Author).

There were several men boarding with the Van Ornums for the journey to Oregon: Judson Cressey, Samuel Gleason, Lewis Lawson, and the two Reith brothers. An old gentleman named Goodsel Munson had loaned Alexis Van Ornum two oxen. In exchange, Munson was also boarding with the Van Ornums through the route.^{ME}

Lewis Lawson was a driver for one of the Van Ornum teams. The two Reith brothers, Germans from Minnesota, also drove two wagons in return for their board. There was Jacob, who was born in France in the Rhineland province of Alsace over twenty years previously, and his brother Joseph. They had immigrated with their family from France in 1850 to New York State, moving on to Minnesota in 1860.[13]

Each of the eight wagons in the Utter train were drawn by two or three yoke of oxen. There were some sixty-four head of oxen to draw on for teams. In addition to the work cattle, the train was accompanied by some fifty head of loose stock. Also there were a few saddle horses and a very valuable draft horse, a black stallion of the breed from the Percheron province of France, which belonged to Mr. Van Ornum.[14]

The parting with the larger California train was a sad time for the Myers. Margaret remembered

the controversy, as mother's brother tried to get father to change his mind and go with him to California, saying the company was now so small their danger from Indian attack would be much greater. Also, mother was his only sister, and their grief at parting was sad. They had left their parents, now growing old, in far off Wisconsin, and I believe Mother had cherished the hope all along that one or the other would give in and keep together, but father was set for Oregon.

The mood of the smaller train was summed up by Emeline:

We were left more lonely than before. We had felt the security of traveling with such a large number. . . . but how soon all changed when we parted with our friends of the California train, and traveled westward, knowing that we were every day nearing the dangerous part of our journey.

But still we kept on over hills, through forests, across mountains and rivers, until we came to Fort Hall, where soldiers were stationed.

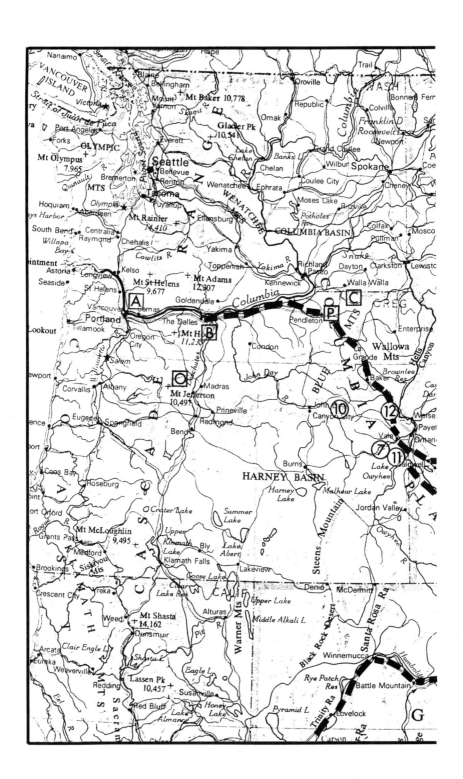

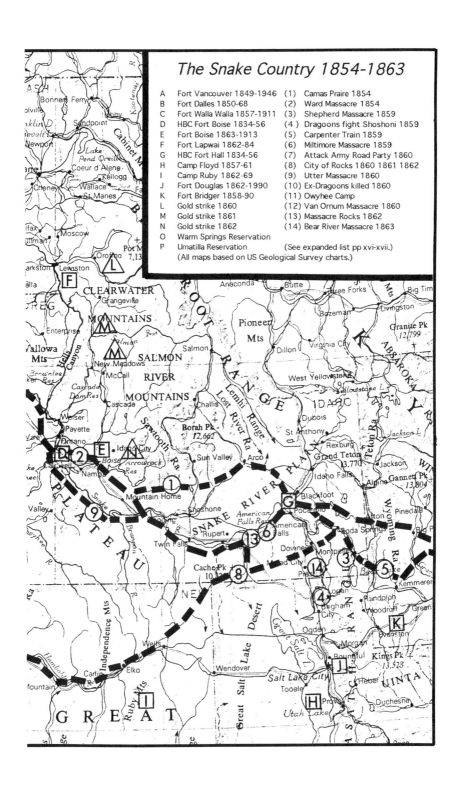

The Snake Country 1854-1863

A	Fort Vancouver 1849-1946	(1) Camas Praire 1854
B	Fort Dalles 1850-68	(2) Ward Massacre 1854
C	Fort Walla Walla 1857-1911	(3) Shepherd Massacre 1859
D	HBC Fort Boise 1834-56	(4) Dragoons fight Shoshoni 1859
E	Fort Boise 1863-1913	(5) Carpenter Train 1859
F	Fort Lapwai 1862-84	(6) Miltimore Massacre 1859
G	HBC Fort Hall 1834-56	(7) Attack Army Road Party 1860
H	Camp Floyd 1857-61	(8) City of Rocks 1860 1861 1862
I	Camp Ruby 1862-69	(9) Utter Massacre 1860
J	Fort Douglas 1862-1990	(10) Ex-Dragoons killed 1860
K	Fort Bridger 1858-90	(11) Owyhee Camp
L	Gold strike 1860	(12) Van Ornum Massacre 1860
M	Gold strike 1861	(13) Massacre Rocks 1862
N	Gold strike 1862	(14) Bear River Massacre 1863
O	Warm Springs Reservation	
P	Umatilla Reservation	(See expanded list pp xvi-xvii.)
	(All maps based on US Geological Survey charts.)	

ts Last Camp In the

NON

JOSEPH MYERS

Photo Taken About 10 Years After the
Massacre Mr. Myers Died in 1884.

MRS. MARY E. MYERS

Wife of Joseph Myers—Photo Taken a
Short Time After the Massacre.

even t this day They knew that a
large part emgrants had escaped
but were more interested in the
stolen property than father massa-
re They frequently rode to the
river for water but hurried back without making any attempt to locate the

meat. It appears then that the three
returned to the camp on the Owyhee
to report the news to their suffering
companions.

Members of the Camp.

From all sources of information ob-
tainable we gather the following as

Joseph & Mary Myers

As pictured in the *Boise Capital News*, 5 December 1915.

TWO

Dragoon Escort

The Utter wagon train arrived in the vicinity of the abandoned Hudson Bay Company trading post of Fort Hall around the evening of 21 August 1860.[1] There they found the soldiers' encampment near the bridge over the Portneuf River. Here the emigrants "heard some talk about danger from marauding bands of Shoshone and Snake* Indians."[MM]

The Utter party had been traveling for several days in the land of the Shoshoni and would continue to travel in their lands while crossing the Snake River plains. The men of the Utter train undoubtedly heard some account of the 1859 massacres. There were three major attacks on emigrant trains the previous year. Although these assaults were made by Indians, each of them were led by or involved white men. The first was the attack on the Shepherd Train at the end of July 1859 in the Bear River area (either on the Hudspeth or Sublette Cutoffs): four men were killed outright and one mortally wounded.

The Army District of Utah was headquartered at Camp Floyd, located forty miles to the south of Salt Lake City. A dragoon force under the command of Lieutenant Ebenezer Gay was dispatched from Camp Floyd to apprehend the perpetrators of the "Shepherd Massacre." While enroute to Bear River, this force had a fight with Shoshoni Indians in Box Elder canyon (between Brigham City and Cache Valley). A larger

---

*The Snake River country is the large region drained by the Snake and its tributaries, which includes watersheds in five states adjoining Idaho (but not Montana). The *Snake Country* was that portion of the Snake River country inhabited by the *Snakes*: central and southern Idaho and areas of adjacent states. Although *Snake* was a term used for all Shoshoni, it generally applied to the Northern Shoshoni and Bannnocks centered on the Snake River Plains, and also some Northern Paiute of eastern Oregon. The northern part of the Snake River country was peopled by the Nez Perce and Coeur d'Alene.

force out of Camp Floyd, under Major Lynde, operated to the
west along the Humboldt. The Humboldt River expedition
joined Lieutenant Gay's force at the emigrant ford over the
Bear River. These troops formed the Bear River Expedition
and were no sooner joined by additional forces from Camp
Floyd when another train was ambushed.

On 20 August 1859 the Carpenter train was attacked in a
canyon in the general vicinity of the previous attack on emigrants. One man was killed outright and three others seriously
wounded; the wagon train had to be abandoned. The presence
of the troops on the trails did not forestall a third assault. This,
the most heineous of the attacks on emigrant trains, occurred
on the last day of August to the west of Fort Hall. Seven
members of the Miltimore family plus another individual were
killed.*

As the season of travel came to a close in 1859, the army
district of Utah had instituted an escort system for the wagon
trains. Because of the attacks, Captain Wallen's Wagon Road
Expedition from the district of Oregon waited at Raft River,
and then escorted the last trains over the Snake River plains on
the return to Oregon.

For 1860 the district of Utah positioned troops at several
encampments along the California and Oregon routes. They
sent out patrols and escorted trains. The district of Oregon had
troops under Major Grier patrolling along the Oregon Trail to
the west of Salmon Falls. Operating to the west of Major Grier
was the central Oregon wagon road expedition of Major Enoch
Steen; Captain A. L. Smith commanded an eastern portion of
the force to the east of Lake Harney. Some twenty miles from
the Malheur river on 23 June, the end of Smith's column was
attacked by an Indian war party in an attempt to stampede the
army horses and mules. In response to this brazen act, Major
Steen combined his and Smith's forces into an 'Expedition
Against the Snake Indians,' secured reinforcements and additional provisions, and scoured eastern Oregon in a search for

---

*See the author's *The Boise Massacre* for a detailed account of the 1859 massacres, army expeditions,
and Shoshoni.

the hostile Indians. At the headwaters of the Malheur they found the camp where a party of miners had been attacked on 13 June by "hostile Indians and completely routed." By mid-August Major Steen had come to believe that "but very few Indians inhabit the Country, through which I have recently scouted and these are secreted, in small individual families, in rocks and bushes."[2] He was referring to Northern Paiute country, but was in general agreement with his officers that the marauders were Snakes from the Snake River plains.

The soldiers on escort duty at the Portneuf were aware of the danger of Indian attacks in the Snake Country, but probably had not yet learned of any occurring in 1860. Already that summer, members of at least two wagon trains could attest to the hostile activity of the Snake Indians.

] An Attack Along The Snake [

Like the Utters and Myers, the Wiley and Norton families were also neighbors from Wisconsin and emigrating to the Willamette Valley. One of the Norton boys was Walter (he later lived in Portland). Joseph L. and Matilda Batcheldor Wiley had their seven children with them. One of their boys (C. B. Wiley, who later lived at Tillamook) turned fourteen that June. The Wileys and the Nortons traveled together in a wagon train ahead of the Utter train. They crossed the Missouri River at Council Bluffs and kept on the north side of the Platte. C. B. Wiley later recalled that one night, as they crossed the Snake Country, Mr. Norton

was on night guard. We were camped on the banks of the Snake River. It was a starless, moonless night. He had a fine riding mare, and a 3-year-old from the mare. An Indian crept up through the darkness, caught and mounted the mare and made off. Norton jumped on the three-year-old and took after him. Strain his ears as he would, Mr. Norton could not hear the hoofbeats of the stolen mare. He rode on. The colt nickered and the mare answered. He gave the colt its head and it joined its mother. The mare had a halter on. Just as he grabbed the halter the Indian let fly an arrow. The steel arrow lodged in Norton's arm. He broke the shaft of the arrow off close to his arm. The Indian slipped off the mare and got away in the darkness.

The next day as we were eating lunch seven Indians came into camp, begging for food. Our men folks paid no attention to them. All but one of them left, and a moment or so later the dry grass on all sides of us was ablaze. The Indian who had stayed in camp jumped up and, waving his blanket, dashed at our stock to stampede them. The other six charged into camp, waving blankets and shouting to stampede our cattle. Some of the men ran to where the frightened cattle were about to break away, while others ran for their guns. The Indians vamoosed and our men quieted the cattle.

Next day at noon seven other Indians came into our camp to sell buckskin. One of their number, their leader, had a cut across his face that extended from his eyebrow to his chin. We yoked up and started on. As we started down a draw my father saw an Indian peering over the brow of a nearby hill. We had with us a French Canadian, a former trapper and mountain man. He told us to corral in a hurry. More than 100 Indians poured over the brow of the hill, but we were ready for them so they gave us up as a bad job.[3]

As the Utter wagon train at Fort Hall prepared to cross the Snake River plains, far to the west at the edge of the Snake Country Major Steen reported from his camp on the meadows just north of Malheur Lake:

> Head Quarters, Expedition against Snake
> Indians, Camp on Big Meadows.
> August 23, 1860
> . . . a large Indian trail was discovered in the vicinity

of my camp; I at once dispatched Capt: A. J. Smith, 1st Dragoons, with eighty Dragoons of Cos: "C" and "H" in pursuit of the Indians who had passed over it. Captain Smith's command arrived here yesterday, having been absent three days. The Captain reports that he followed a large trail for some miles Northward of this valley, but on reaching the mountains, the main trail was broken into several smaller ones, and that the Indians had dispersed in different directions; he kept up the pursuit as long as a trail could be found for one hundred miles.

The Dragoon horses requiring rest, I will make the following change in the plan of my operations, presented in my Report of the 18th inst: I will dispatch three columns from this camp in the direction of the Blue Mountains and head waters of Crooked River. These columns will move upon lines about twenty miles distant from each other, and will make a thorough search of the mountainous country Northward. The supply trains will move by the wagon road to Crooked River where my entire command will be on about the 5th of September, and from which point I will, if not other wise ordered, proceed to the Dalles.[4]

] Army Escort To Rock Creek [

It is doubtful that the men of the Utter train wished to alarm the children and women by passing on much, if any, of what had been learned of the 1859 massacres. So, to thirteen-year-old Emeline Timble, it seemed that it was the emigrant's idea to have an army escort. "As we deemed it unsafe to go farther alone, we called for troops to go with us." One group of dragoons had already gone with a train just a few days ahead. The emigrants had to wait for the soldiers to make preparations for the escort that would safely see them through the dangerous area.[5]

August - November 1860

	Su	M	Tu	W	Th	F	Sa
Aug	19	20	21 Arrive Ft. Hall.	22	23 Leave Ft. Hall with Escort.	24 Escort Day 2.	25 Day 3.
	26 Day 4.	27 Day 5.	28 Day 6.	29 Escort Returns.	30	31	1
Sept	2	3	4	5	6	7	8 Arrive at Castle Butte.
	9 Wagon train attacked	10 Wagon train abandoned.	11	12	13	14 Indians stop following.	15
	16	17 Munson & Christy go on ahead.	18 Arrive at Owyhee R. Stop travel.	19	20	21	22 Group meet on the Malheur R.
	23	24	25	26	27	28	29
Oct	30 Snyder found at Willow Ck.	1 Cole letter. Indians first visit Owyhee.	2 Reith brothers reach Umatilla Res.	3	4 Van Ornums leave. Mr. Chase dies.	5 Mr. Chase buried.	6
	7 Indians last visit at Owyhee Camp	8	9	10	11	12	13 Libbie dies.
	14	15	16	17	18 Susan dies.	19 Munson & C rescued. Danny dies.	20
	21 Albert dies.	22	23	24 Advance troops reach Owyhee.	25 Dent & main force reach Owyhee.	26	27 Expedition departs Owyhee R.
Nov	28	29	30	31	1	2	3
	4	5	6	7 Expedition reaches Ft. Walla Walla.	8 Captain Dent's Army Report.	9	10 Myers family to The Dalles.
	11	12 Myers family reach Portland.	13	14	15	16	17

Calendar of the Utter Disaster.   (Compiled by Author).

The soldiers at Fort Hall belonged to the regiment of 2nd Dragoons which was stationed at the huge military post of Camp Floyd in Utah Territory. After a harsh winter in Utah, Lieutenant Colonel Marshall Saxe Howe had brought Companies B, E, and H of the 2nd Dragoons to an encampment at the bridge across the Portneuf River. This was on the Oregon Trail near the abandoned fur trading post of Fort Hall. The dragoons had arrived at the Portneuf 21 June. They had been engaged in scouting the country during the remainder of the month. In July and August the dragoons continuously escorted emigrants on the Trails: from 100 miles east of the Portneuf River, to the west to Rock Creek and Salmon Falls, and up Raft River on the California Trail to the City of Rocks near the border of Utah Territory. On 22 August Colonel Howe wrote to Headquarters, District of Utah:

> Camp on Left Bank Port Neuf River, W.T., Hq 2nd Dragoons. . . . report scouts enroute to Salt River, 100 miles East [on Lander Road], and to City of Rocks 93 miles, and to Salmon falls 140 miles west, and have not heard of any disturbance by Indians till the 16th inst. . . . man wounded at Bluffs 15 m East of Salt River.[6]

The Army's Annual Return of 1860 showed that the 'Port Neuf Emigrant Route Expedition W.T.' had two deaths and a number of desertions, with some deserters being apprehended. The three dragoon companies had five deserters for the month of August alone. There were also some troopers who were discharged from the Army that month as their five-year enlistments expired.

Five of the discharged soldiers, from Company B, were heading for Oregon and wanted to join the Utter train. The emigrants "decided to equip them with saddle horses and guns in order that they might act as guards or scouts in return for the sustenance supplied them."[7] The last of these troopers to be discharged were Privates William Utley and Theodore Murdock whose enlistments expired 23 August. Murdock (or Murdoch), now age twenty-four, had enlisted at Fort Belknap; he was a farmer, born in Baltimore. The other three were Privates Henry Snyder and Charles Kishnell and Sergeant Charles Schamberg. Sergeant Schamberg was twenty-seven, born in Hess Cassell, Germany. He had enlisted in Cleveland,

Ohio. Henry Snyder was older, twenty-nine. He had been a mason by occupation who enlisted in St. Louis but was born in Lenning or Lenne, Germany.[8]   The five all had money or checks; each had some $400 to $700. Some soldiers had gotten their discharge checks cashed at Camp Floyd (Snyder had not cashed his).[M]

When the Utter Train first arrived at the Portneuf, old Mr. Munson of the Van Ornum Party changed his mind and wanted to go to California. He demanded his oxen, or at least complained to Lieutenant Colonel Howe, the Army commander at the Portneuf encampment. The Colonel rode down to the emigrant camp and arbitrarily demanded or commanded the oxen to be delivered to Mr. Munson. This caused ill feeling among the emigrants toward the Colonel.[M]

While waiting, the first evening or the following one, Colonel Howe sent an invitation to the women and girls of the train to attend a dance, to be held in the soldiers' tent area. Some of the women refused the request, but Colonel Howe insisted and even advised several of the ladies to go in opposition to the wishes of their husbands. Although some women did attend the dance, others declined the invitation, displeasing the Colonel. Colonel Howe, piqued at the slight, swore the train should have no military escort.[E][M]

At first Colonel Howe refused to send any of his men with the emigrants, but he reconsidered as he did not dare to refuse an escort. The escort of twenty-two dragoons was furnished with only twelve days rations, and (Emeline thought) had instructions not to go as far with this train as the escort sent with the train ahead had gone. The dragoons were to join the train at the Portneuf River crossing, seven miles west of the abandoned Fort Hall. The soldiers would escort the train for six days along the Trail and then return. The emigrants requested protection over a greater part of the road. They were informed by Colonel Howe that there would be no trouble; there were troops on the roads beyond Salmon Falls from the Army posts in Oregon and Washington. He advised the Utter party that they were in no danger if they would not allow the Indians to come too near to their camp. Colonel Howe still seemed to have some prejudice against the Utter party, and showed contempt for their apprehensions. So, after his advice as to how they should manage the Indians, he sent the emigrants on their way.[ME]

Colonel Howe was generally disliked by the Utter party. He furnished an escort for a California-bound sheep train, but for what distance the emigrants did not know. (Many in Oregon held the opinion that the California route was never considered half as dangerous as the Oregon road.)[M]

Emeline Trimble noted that "we found the Indians meant mischief, as they did not come to our wagons, but would occasionally come in sight at a distance; seemed to be watching us, and acted as though they were not friendly to us." The emigrants were told by the soldiers of the escort that they "apprehended danger," and said that the "train was doomed." The Lieutenant commanding the escort expressed his opinion to that effect. The Lieutenant could not violate his orders, which were strict and to the point: the dragoons were to escort the emigrants for six days only, which they did.[ME]

The troopers went a distance of 110 miles from the Portneuf crossing, to a point about three days of travel above Salmon Falls. This would put the escort and train along Rock Creek, just a couple of miles short of the creek's natural crossing (two miles southeast of Twin Falls, Idaho). From this camp the troops returned to the Fort Hall area; they had accompanied the emigrants as far as the supply of rations allowed.[9]

When they turned back, the officer in charge of the escort told the emigrants that they were now out of the danger zone. He felt it was unlikely the wagon train would have any trouble from the Shoshoni from there on, as troops patrolling from the Boise area would probably meet the Utter party. In any event, the Lieutenant thought, the presence of the Oregon troops around the old Fort Boise would overawe the Indians so the wagon trains would pass safely.[M] The soldiers of the escort continued their joshing of the emigrants, and told them that the train was "just in the edge of danger." So they found it, for the "Indians were even then at hand."[ME]

]   To Castle Butte   [

The Utter train crossed Rock Creek the next day.   The
emigrants found that one of the dragoons had deserted and
wanted to go with the Utter party. He was Lucius M. Chaffee,
the young bugler of Company E, 2nd Dragoons. He had enlisted three years earlier at Carlisle, Pennsylvania at age fifteen.
Back then, the five-foot three-inch, blue eyed, sandy-haired
enlistee with the fair complexion had given his name as Lucius
Chaffee. His birthplace, Parkman, Ohio. The Army listed him
as deserting 29 August 1860 while on detached duty. Chaffee
took his bugle with him, but the emigrant party did not enjoy
his music as well as they did before, when they had felt safer.[10]

With the cavalry escort gone, the emigrants discussed the
warnings of the soldiers. The Indians began visiting the wagons, and when they came, it was almost always in groups of
less than ten. The Indians seemed friendly enough but were so
curious the emigrants thought they might be spying.

Even though the emigrants were not being molested by the
Indians, Joseph Myers "felt very bad as the indications were
ominous."[11]   Emeline Trimble elaborated on this, describing
how they camped late one night at the end of August.

> We had not been in camp long when three Indians and
> two Squaws came into camp and all agreed that the
> leader among them must be a white man, as his dress
> and appearance was different from the rest. He had a
> beard, and you could plainly see he was painted. He
> wore an old white hat, with the top of the crown gone,
> we could tell him as far as we could see him, he was
> so different from the rest. They stayed around our
> wagons until late, when our men told them they must
> go to their homes, as we wished to go to bed. They
> waited to be told a number of times, and finally went
> away.

This Indian leader (or renegade white man)* was also described by Joseph Myers, as "being of medium size, rather
slim, blind in one eye, with long hair, generally pulled down
over the blind eye, with considerable beard, especially on the
upper lip." When the Indian visited the emigrant's camp, the
train was either along Rock Creek or to the west of it.

After Rock Creek the route of the Oregon Trail passed over
high ground above the canyon, then descended to the Snake
River before crossing Deep Creek and Salmon Falls River.[12]
Emeline continued:

> We started early next morning, and did not go far be-
> fore we came to good feed and water, and as we had a
> dry camp the night before, the men decided to stop
> part of the day and water and feed the teams and stock,
> and let the women wash. In a short time the same In-
> dians came to us, talked awhile, and told us they were
> going off into the mountains to hunt, and said good-
> bye, and left us. We were suspicious of them, and the
> men consulted together, and thought the safest way
> would be to kill them, but hardly dared to do so, for
> fear of its being found out by the Indians. Still, we
> thought them spies, and I often wish that we had done
> as our better judgement told us, and killed them and
> secreted the bodies, but it seemed it was not to be so.
> All went well . . . .
>
> We saw no Indians to alarm us, and had almost
> regained our cheerfulness, and were very hopeful that
> our fears were unfounded, when on reaching Salmon
> Falls, on the Snake River, who should we meet but
> our supposed white man and the two Indians who
> were with him before, and a number of other Indians
> with them. They came to our wagons and pretended
> to be glad to see us. We bought some dried salmon of
> them, and hurried away, thankful to be rid of them,

---

*A good discussion of the role that 'white Indians' or renegade white men played in the depredations on
the overland trails is contained in John D. Unruh's chapter on "Emigrant-Indian Interaction" in *The Plains A-
cross* and in Brigham D. Madsen's *Shoshoni Frontier and the Bear River Massacre*.

but it worried us as we were followed. We went on
. . . with all quiet . . .

The emigrant party passed Salmon Falls about 2 September. Two days later they left the main Oregon Trail at the Three Island Crossing of the Snake River (Glenns Ferry, Idaho). They followed the alternate route along the south side of the river. After the cavalry escort had left the wagon train at Rock Creek, the Utter Party traveled another 115 miles, to the Bruneau River. This was a more leisurely pace, averaging twelve to fifteen miles per day. The heat became oppressive in the afternoons. As the oxen traveled better in the early morning, the emigrants were up early. During this time nothing of importance occurred, although the attitude of the Indians at Salmon Falls had seemed threatening. Someone did call attention to "a bird call which all thought strange" as they were "traveling through desert and had not seen a bird for a long time. Grass was gone, or nearly so, and only water long distances apart."[13]

Twenty-two miles after crossing the Bruneau River they reached Castle Creek, on Saturday, 8 September. There was often high grass along the small crooked stream and abreast of the castle rock. The creek took its name from Castle Butte which lay east of the stream, "so called from some singular looking rocks having the appearance of old dilapidated castles and other ruins."[14]

The emigrants were able to see this landmark for some distance on the trail and watched the shape of the buttes change as they drew closer. The Snake River lies a half mile north of Castle Butte and flows to the north and west. A half mile northwest of the castle rock and the creek lies another rocky prominence.

In her narrative, Emeline Trimble had confused the Bruneau River with Castle Creek.

There we found a good place for our stock to graze. We always sent a man out with the cattle and horses, for fear they would be stolen, and when our

cattle were brought into camp at night there were one
or two yoke of oxen missing. The men searched for
them and found their tracks where they had been driv-
en up a canyon by Indians. We kept a good watch that
night and were not molested.

The oxen lost to the Indians belonged to Alexis Van
Ornum. In the morning, he insisted on hunting for the cattle as
the remaining three oxen of the team were too poor to pull the
wagon alone. The men hunted awhile for the oxen without
success. Van Ornum threw away everything that he could
spare to lighten the load in the wagon, and someone let him
have a yoke of oxen to hitch with his team. They all started
along the trail with Van Ornum in the lead wagon, his large,
black stallion tied behind. They were alarmed that the Indians
had been able to drive the oxen away so quietly, and they were
feeling glad to leave what seemed to them a dangerous place.[15]

So very quietly and with many forebodings they
started the day's journey.
Morning jokes and laughter were forgotten and si-
lently they went on their way.[MM]

Approaching Castle Butte
High ground to left of Castle Butte is west of Castle Creek. Further left is the rimrock
beyond Henderson Flat and Snake River.   (Photo by Author.)

Closer view of Castle Butte
(Photo courtesey of James H. Oates)

THREE

The Attack on the Utter Train

It was 9 September 1860. The Utter train of eight wagons headed down the trail along Castle Creek. There were forty-four persons with over a hundred head of stock: ox teams, horses, cattle, and stock dogs. They were traveling northwest on the South Alternate portion of the Oregon Trail, called the Dry Route.

> We traveled only a short distance before we came
> to a grave where a man belonging to the train ahead of
> us had been buried, and the Indians had dug him up,
> taken his clothing, and then partly buried him, leaving
> one hand and foot out of the grave. You cannot ima-
> gine what a terror struck our hearts as we gazed on the
> awful sight and reflected that we might share the same
> fate.[E]

On looking about the scene, the emigrant party found bones hung on the trees. This was a notice left by a train that had passed thirteen days earlier. Written upon the bones was a warning of danger. They found writing on a board which was an account of how the dead man came to be killed by the Indians. The man had left the train to go after some stray sheep, and was then killed. There was also a warning to anyone who came that way to be very cautious. Mrs. Utter "expressed her belief that she would not go much farther."[M] The warning came too late to do any good.

The train passed over the hill west of Castle Creek and headed again in the direction of the Snake River. After going about a mile, Alexis Van Ornum noticed a cloud of dust on the

Looking east, across Castle Creek to Castle Butte

High ground west of Castle Creek

trail ahead. He immediately stopped the oxen and climbed to
the top of the wagon to see. The drivers of the wagons behind
noticed his action and hurried forward to determine the cause
of his alarm. The ex-dragoons:

> rode forward and were not slow in discerning that the
> dust in the road ahead was being disturbed by the
> movement of a war party of Indians. On reaching a
> point about one-half mile ahead of the train, it was ob-
> served that the savages were assembling in a slight
> depression behind a knoll, and as the troopers
> concluded, for the purpose of formulating plans of
> attack.
>   . . . Soon a horseman was seen to emerge from
> the swale, halt and carefully observe the emigrants. An
> imposing picture this chieftain made, bedecked in the
> regulation feathered war bonnet: breech cloth, belt,
> scalping knife and rifle. . . .
>   After satisfying himself that conditions were fa-
> vorable he gave the blood curdling war whoop, buried
> his heels in the flanks of his steed and the charge was
> on. Like bees from a hive these naked fiends swarm-
> ed over the hill and up the trail.[1]

Suddenly the emigrants were in full sight of the Indians as
the warriors came over the rolling sand hill toward the wagon
train. There were about one hundred Shoshoni or Bannocks,
most of them on foot. They were singing their war songs.

The emigrants saw at a glance what must be done. Mr.
Utter (who was recognized as the head of the party) and Mr.
Van Ornum in the lead wagon immediately caused the train to
be formed in a corral of wagons for defense. The emigrants
did not think the Indians meant any harm to them. They believed the Indians were only after the horses and cattle. They
drove their stock within the circle and the valuable Percheron
stallion was further protected by forming a barricade of two
wagons. The men got their guns so as to be ready to shoot if
the Indians attempted to harm the emigrants.

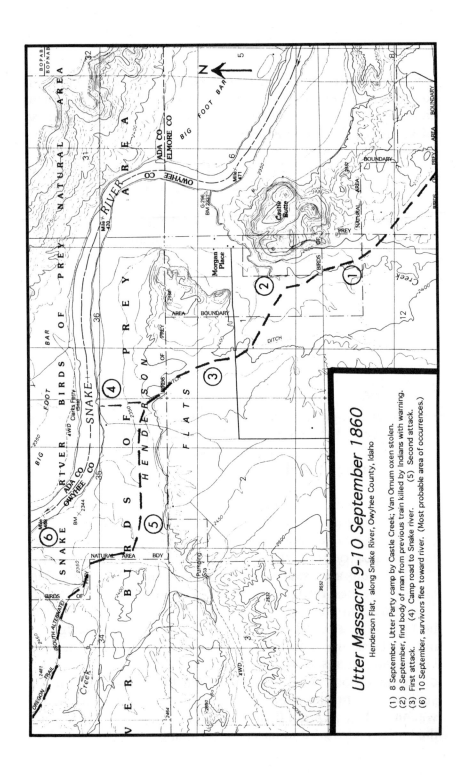

Utter Massacre 9-10 September 1860

Henderson Flat, along Snake River, Owyhee County, Idaho

(1) 8 September, Utter Party camp by Castle Creek; Van Ornum oxen stolen.
(2) 9 September, find body of man from previous train killed by Indians with warning.
(3) First attack.   (4) Camp road to Snake river.   (5) Second attack.
(6) 10 September, survivors flee toward river. (Most probable area of occurrences.)

Accompanied by their many yelping dogs, the Indians, on foot and on horses of every kind, shape, and color, charged the emigrant train. They waved their blankets and buffalo robes while all the time shouting their war whoops. The women and children were repeatedly told to get under cover. In spite of these commands it was impossible for them to resist the temptation to witness the drama. Every eye was riveted on the appalling scene before them. The dust arose in clouds as the soil of the desert and the roadway was churned by the clattering hoofs of the Indian ponies. To thirteen-year-old Emeline Trimble, the Indian's

> shrill war whoops I can never forget. It was too terrible to even attempt to describe, but suffice it to say that although so many years have elapsed since that awful, awful scene, I can never hear a shrill yell without shirking with much the feelings which I experienced as that terrible noise reached our ears.

It was between nine and ten o'clock that the Snake Indians first surrounded the train. They whooped and yelled in an attempt to stampede the stock. They did not succeed and did little damage. The emigrants held a favorable position, but had no water. They had eighteen men and boys capable of bearing arms, and were well armed. There were also five women, and twenty-one children between the ages of one and fourteen years.

For awhile the Indians kept up their attack, but could accomplish nothing against the corralled train. They found the location unsuitable for a battle and had failed to stampede the stock. After a time, about an hour, they threw down their arms and proffered friendship by holding up their hands in sign of peace. The Chief rode up and down the road waving a white cloth and motioning that the emigrants could go on at noon. The men allowed two or three of the Indians to come up close to the wagons as the warriors had motioned that they wanted to talk. Some of the men went out and met them. By the use of many signs and such English words as "me good Indian" and "me friend Boston man," it was indicated that the Indians were a war party and wanted to be fed. They said they would not hurt the emigrants, that the Indians were only hungry, and that the train was to go on after nooning. Margaret Myers told how the Indians

> made the men understand they wanted to make a treaty. As always, some were in favor and some were not. They said we could go on if we gave them a certain amount of flour, sugar, and other food. Father opposed it, saying it was a trap. They had gone too far and intended to fight as they were naked and in war paint.

The men decided it would be prudent to buy the Indians' favor by giving them food. All of the Indians that came into the corralled wagons were fed. Although the Indians appeared to be satisfied, that dinner time did not find the emigrants with their accustomed appetites. After some talking by signs, indicating that they were friendly Indians and that the emigrants might pass on to the river for water, the Indians drew off and rode peacefully away. The wagon train started along the trail again, supposedly toward the river. Mrs. Myers related that: "Believing our trouble over . . . we thanked God for our deliverance and, as we saw the Indians depart, felt free to resume our journey."[2]

] Second Attack [

The main trail continued on parallel to the river, but a 'camp road' turned down to the river which was a quarter of a mile further. By the river was a beautiful meadow of about forty acres with the river running by and a perpendicular cliff many hundreds of feet high on the other side. (This was a good place to camp and was well protected from attack on all sides, with plenty of grass and water.)[3] After the emigrants got out of their strong position and strung out on the trail (following their nooning), they expected some kind of treachery from these Snake Indians and were on the lookout for them. They did not take the side road that the Indians expected, but instead kept up the hill from them. The last wagon had hardly started before the Indians again commenced their terrible war songs and dancing, coming toward the train all the while.

The wagon train traveled up a piece of high ground with a slight ravine on each side of the road. There was tall, thick sagebrush on either side and fifty yards away the sagebrush grew as high as a man's head. Meanwhile, some of the Indians rode on ahead, sent their horses out of sight, and, of course, took possession of those ravines. When the emigrants reached the top of this eminence, Alexis Van Ornum saw the form of an Indian emerge. An instant later he heard the crack of a rifle. The train had become exposed to the fire from ambushing Indians who were dismounted and hiding in the cover of the sagebrush. In their attack, the Indians shot at the cattle with their bows and arrows and succeeded in wounding some of them. At the same time they tried to again stampede the horses and cattle. The emigrants attempted to drive the wagons on. At the foot of the hill the Indians surrounded the wagon train and began firing at the emigrants with guns.

The Utter party again corralled the wagons as quickly as they could, but in the meantime, some of the oxen were hit with arrows. Some of the stock had as many as three or four arrows sticking in them. This time the Indians were using guns as well as bows. Before the last wagon could be put in place, the man driving it was shot dead. He was Lewis Lawson from Iowa, who was with the Van Ornums. Also, before the corral was completed and the ox teams chained, another of the men was felled by a shot. He was the recently discharged soldier, Private William Utley, who fell just beside the Myers' wagon. Then, shortly after the first two men were shot, a second discharged dragoon was shot down. He was a German, Private Charles Kishnel. (Another of the discharged soldiers, Henry Snyder, took his fallen companions' money and papers afterwards, in the presence of the emigrants.)

Where South Alternate Trail entered Henderson Flat
Snake River in the distance.

Looking over western part of Henderson Flat

It was about eleven in the morning. The emigrants had placed their eight wagons in a circle. The men piled supplies between the wagons so they could fight from behind the improvised breastworks. Mrs. Myers had heard that feather beds were a protection against bullets. She rolled their beds from the bottom of the wagon box and placed them to the side of the wagon nearest the attackers. She gathered her children about her to await developments.

The wary Indians encircled the wagons at a safe distance and fired a few rifle shots at the emigrants. They then commenced a general firing upon the wagon train with arrows and rifles. Before long they closed in around the circled wagons and sent a shower of arrows into the stockade while the rifle bullets riddled the wagon covers. The members of the wagon train defended themselves as well as they could. The women and children sought what shelter they could in the wagon boxes. The wagons were in a fairly open space. The men dug shallow trenchs that they could drop into while reloading or cooling their guns. No one had time to help William Utley who was wounded in the chest. He finally managed to crawl under the Myers' wagon to get out of the sun.

The fighting continued through the day as the Indians circled around the wagons, firing at them. The emigrants picked off Indians whenever they got a chance. Occasionally an Indian would ride too close and would be shot down by the fire from the men defending the wagons. Several Indians were killed during this first day of fighting. Joseph Myers estimated the number at about twenty or more.[4] This September day was very hot:

> The plaintive voices of the children could be heard calling for water, a call that filled the very souls of the parents with anguish. The hideous yell of the naked savage, barking of dogs, the bellowing of suffering cattle as they surged back and forth within the inclosure, the blood gushing from bullet wounds, arrows fastened in their sides and the long shafts swaying

with every movement: the groans of the fallen defenders and the cries of the women made an indelible impression on the memory of those who [survived].[5]

The emigrants continued fighting the Indians all that afternoon and evening. Now there were more rifles in the hands of the attackers as more Indians arrived, swelling their numbers. There was no moon, but it was a clear night. By starlight, Joseph Myers "distinctly saw a white man, mounted on a large horse . . . he raised and aimed his rifle at him but he slipped away in the dark before he had time to fire. He always regretted this as he was convinced at the time, and ever afterward, that it was a Mormon leader."[MM]

During that long, awful night the defenders watched for an opportunity to get away under the cover of darkness. There was none. If the Indians heard the least noise they would commence whooping and shooting at the train. They kept up the shooting at intervals through the night; mostly with arrows, occasionally with rifles. They had just a few guns but plenty of arrows. The Indians' random shots did not do much harm except to wound and irritate the cattle and horses, which were quite restless from being without grass and water all day and night. The attackers were not deliberately shooting at the stock as they wanted the animals alive.

William Utley died sometime during the night. Margaret Myers remembered "stooping and looking through a small crack in the floor of the wagon bed and seeing his dead face." Some of the cows were in the enclosure and they were milked. The milk was given to the babies and the smaller children. Only the younger children were able to close their eyes in sleep that night.

The fighting was renewed in the morning (10 September). The Indians charged at daybreak but were stood off. They continued to circle around the wagons, shooting as they rode by. The fight continued through the day. Another man, Judson Cressey of the Van Ornum party, was killed. Isabella Myers' mother had taken our feather beds and fastened them up inside the cover of our wagon. The arrows would go into the feather beds but would not come clear through. I looked through the cracks in the bottom of our wagon bed and saw a man all covered with blood lying very still. I asked mother about him, and she said he was dead— that the Indians had killed him with a stray shot. We children could hardly stand the heat. It was a blazing hot day, and there was no air stirring. The feather beds kept out all the air.

It was very warm weather and the emigrants were all nearly famished for water. The previous morning, the first day of the attack, they had not filled the water kegs as usual since they knew they would travel along the river. But now, their cattle had become almost unmanageable from starvation, thirst, and being wounded by arrows.

From the second attack on the first day, through the night, and all the next day until dusk, the men defending the wagons had little food or drink. The women and children aided the men as much as they could. They soaked bread in water and threw it down to the men within reach, as the men fought in the shallow trenches. The women and children also loaded guns and revolvers and handed them down to the men, and then reloaded the emptied weapons. The women protected the children as much as they could.

There were just too many Indians attacking the wagon train. Some of the emigrants had defended themselves about thirty hours without a drop of water, in which time four men were killed and some of the party wounded. Mr. Chase and Mr. Utter were both wounded, with Mr. Utter in serious condition. The men were cramped from lying in the shallow trenches. They were quite weary, having had no rest.

The Indians now had closed to within a few feet of the wagons. The emigrants' situation seemed almost hopeless. Another hour and it would be sundown. They were compelled to go to water somehow and the river was "about 100 rods" away.[6]

---

9 September 1860 (Su, Day 1)
   Lewis Lawson
   Ex-Private William Utley
   Ex-Private Charles Kishnell   German
10 September (M, Day 2)
   Judson Cressey
   John W. Myers
   Mary Utter   about 23
   Elijah Utter
   Wesley Utter   5
   Emma Utter
   Abagel Trimble Utter   33
   Abby Utter

Killed In The Attack On the Utter Train.

]   Breakout Attempt   [

The emigrants talked it over and made up their minds that they were all to die. Some loose stock had been driven off by the Indians, but the ox-teams had been tied inside the corral where the rest of the loose stock was. So far, not one of the animals had been killed. The emigrants thought they would try leaving all the wagons but four, one for each family. They would start on, taking some provisions and leaving as booty for the Indians all the stock and other property plus the remaining wagons and their contents. It was hoped that this tactic would entice the attackers and satisfy them for a short time. Thus, while the Indians were plundering the four wagons, the emigrant might escape with the remainder.[7]

The ex-dragoons volunteered to act as skirmishers in front of the wagons, to keep the Indians engaged. So, it was arranged that these three remaining discharged soldiers and the deserter be well armed and mounted on the Van Ornum horses. The four would go in advance to clear the road of Indians and

open the way for the wagons to get to the river. Some of the
ox teams were hitched to the families' wagons. The Reith
brothers no longer had ox teams to drive; they were also
selected to act as a vanguard. The Reiths were to proceed
ahead on foot behind the four mounted men to help drive the
attackers back, to keep the road open, and the Indians from
closing in ahead. According to Isabella Myers:

> Towards evening of the second day the Indians
> agreed that if we would leave four of our wagons and
> supplies they would let us go on. The men hastily re-
> arranged the loads. Hitching the oxen to the remaining
> four wagons, we started on. Most of the Indians
> swarmed about the four wagons we had left, but some
> of them followed us.

Once again the wagon train started out, but after leaving
the corral, the cattle could not be driven on account of their
hunger. They could hardly be moved along as they would
keep biting and reaching at every spear of grass.

The plan to entice the Indians did not succeed. What was
left did not seem to satisfy them at all. As the train began to
move the Indians paid no attention to the deserted wagons but
swarmed about the train like bees, attacking it with renewed
activity.

As the attempt was made to drive off from the corral, John
Myers was driving the team while his brother, Joseph, was
walking along with his gun and revolver. Joseph saw an Indian about fifty yards distant raise up behind a big sage bush
and level his piece at one of the brothers. Joseph raised his
gun, but the Indian's went off first. The next instant Joseph
returned the fire and the Indian gave a whoop, jumped up, and
rolled over dead, but the Indian's shot had hit John Myers who
fell dead without a struggle.

As the Indians pitched in on all sides, the four mounted ex-
dragoons—instead of staying and assisting the emigrants—put
spurs to the horses, charged through the Indians, and galloped
off for dear life. Since the Indians were then dismounted, the

John W. Myers

Killed when the attempt was made to drive off from the corralled wagons on the second
day of the attack on the Utter train.   (By permission from Frank L. Tyler, Nampa, Idaho.)

fleeing ex-soldiers easily succeeded in making their escape.
They rode off as fast as they could go, without firing a shot,
making no resistance whatever, thus leaving the rest to the
mercy of the Indians.   Schamberg, Murdock, Snyder, and
Chaffee were well armed with rifles and revolvers which, with
the horses, belonged to the emigrants.   (The Indians had few
guns and Joseph Myers later believed that if those men had
stayed, the wagon train could have gotten through to water and
been defended until assistance arrived.)

After those mounted on horses in the vanguard had fled, the Indians seemed redoubled in their frenzy They showered such a continual fire upon the train that it seemed impossible for anyone to escape.

There were no less than twenty-five to thirty Indians killed while they had the emigrants hemmed up. It was certain death to an Indian if he showed his head as the defenders were all pretty good marksmen. "The Indians would come right up to the wagons, cut holes in the covers, and shoot their arrows in at the women and children—but few of those who were so bold as to thus come up got away without getting a shot."⁴ One boy killed eight or ten Indians with his rifle. This may have been Charles Utter, a lad, who shot five Indians as fast as he could load and shoot. He was in the rear wagon. His stepsister, Emeline, also defended the wagon for some time, with an ax in hand.

Those left in the train resisted to their utmost. They tried to drive on as fast as they could, fighting their way, but the cattle were so ravenous after the sagebrush along the trail that they could not be driven along. In the meantime, the firing of arrows and rifle balls by the Indians was actively continued. Mr. Utter's wound was so serious that he could do nothing. It was getting dark; the emigrants' resistance weakened; the cattle were hungry; traveling slowed.

] Wagon Train Abandoned [

So many of the men were now gone or disabled that the Utter party could not get the teams along and protect themselves at the same time. The bolder Indians had commenced to survey the booty by thrusting their heads through the openings they cut in the canvas wagon covers. As the Indians began clambering into the wagons the emigrants held a hasty consultation. They decided to leave everything, the cattle and the wagons, and go on foot as best they could.⁸

The men helped the families out of the wagons. Joseph Myers stepped to the side of the wagon and called to his wife,

"Get out, Mary, and we will try to all die together."ᴹᴹ Isabella Myers noticed an Indian cutting a hole in the canvas wagon cover, then saw him poke his head through the opening. She would never forget the look on his face as he glanced from one end of the wagon box to the other. Isabella scrambled out of the wagon.[9] Mary Utter was in the Myers' wagon too.* As Isabella jumped to the ground she was explaining to Mary what she had seen. Just as Joseph Myers was helping Mary Utter out of the wagon and was setting her down, a rifle ball passed through his coat and two shirts, grazed his side, and set fire to some matches in his vest pocket. The shot continued on, into Mary's breast. She fell, but got up again, and cried out, "O, my God! I'm shot!" She called on some of the men to help her. Two young men took hold of her and helped her along a little way, but she "commenced sinking and was getting helpless." She spoke a few words: remarking that she had got her death blow; that she was killed.ᴹ

Joseph Myers helped all of his family from the wagon. He was still shooting as his wife and five children followed him about. Confusion ensued; the women and children were panic stricken as the Indians rushed up on both sides. The attackers were all about the wagons. There were so many of them that at times Joseph Myers could not see Mr. Chase who was standing not more than fifteen feet away.

The families had tried to stay together. As Margaret Myers recalled, it:

> was now nearly dark. The Indians had rushed in and were slashing the canvas covers from the wagons and indulging in a free for all fight among themselves for the loot. All this time we were still following father about, mother with the baby, now about ten months old in her arms, we children staying together, I know not how. Those of us who had learned much in the last two days and realized our danger, expecting to be killed but making no outcry. Even the little lame three year old sister, bravely toddling on patient and still. In

*See Chapter 1 note, p 7.

all that followed I do not recall that any of us cried or whined. It seemed we knew our parents were helpless and could do nothing for us. Had they had the least idea of escaping at this time they could probably have taken something to help them somewhat, but they did not. As they walked about, others, in their despair and frenzy, joined them, and soon a little band of twenty-one or two, mostly children, found themselves on the outskirts of the yelling, fighting horde, and apparently unnoticed.

During this time, Elijah Utter had his baby (one year old that day) in his arms. As Emeline stepped up and took Susan from him—so he could better use his gun—she kissed her stepfather. Emeline and her mother had started away from the wagons just as Mary Utter was shot. Elijah Utter proposed to surrender. He attempted to parley with the Indians and went toward them, holding up his hands as a sign he wanted to talk. He made signs that they might have everything if they would only spare the lives of the surviving members of the party. While Emeline was turned to her mother, who had stopped and was bending over the dying Mary Utter, Elijah was shot in the breast and fell. Emeline and her mother had started again and were off some twenty or thirty steps when Mr. Utter fell. He got up, but immediately fell again, close to his daughter Mary, and died. So the emigrants gave up on them and had to leave Mary, who was about twenty-three years old.

Emeline Trimble, trying to encourage her mother in making their escape, picked up the youngest Utter child, the infant Susan. Emeline was running ahead, the little Utter boy running by her side. She called to her mother to follow. Others told Mrs. Utter that her husband was dead, that she should keep with them. She shook her head, refusing to leave her husband. Mrs. Utter turned back to try to reach Elijah and the three smaller Utter children followed. Emeline turned to see her mother standing by the dead bodies of Elijah and Mary. Emeline begged her to go with them. Mrs. Utter said no, there was no use in trying, they were all to be killed, and she would not leave her husband.

When Emeline realized that she could not persuade her mother to go, she "took one last lingering look at her dear" mother's face. Taking her little baby sister, Susan, in her arms, Emeline told the other four of the little brothers and sisters to follow her and started off, she knew not where, "but with the one hope of getting away from the wretches who seemed to thirst for the blood of everyone" of them. She again turned and motioned to her mother, who still stood back toward the wagon with the two little Utter girls and the little boy. Mrs. Utter shook her head. Then, as the older girl, Emma, started to go to Emeline, she was shot down. Wesley, the boy of five years, was shot and seen to fall upon the lifeless body of his father. Then Mrs. Utter and the other little girl, Abby, were killed. All were seen to fall by the shots of the Indians around the dead body of Elijah Utter. Emeline had turned and run a little farther away; when she looked back again, her mother and the three Utter children had all been felled and were lying with the rest of the dead.[EM] To Emeline:

> It seemed as though our whole dependence had been taken from us, and leaving our wagons, we started, each one for himself. . . . I felt then that all that I held dear on earth was dependent upon my feeble care, and child as I was, I nerved myself for that terrible struggle for life which I could see was before me. . . . pause a moment and reflect upon my situation. A child of barely thirteen years, and slender in build and constitution, taking a nursing babe of one years, and four other children, all younger than herself and fleeing for life without provisions and barely clothing enough to cover us, into the pathless wilderness or what is worse yet, across the barren plains of the west. It was now the 10th day of September, and getting dark, the second day of the attack. Others also fled.

As the remaining emigrants hastened off on foot from the wagons, the Indians fell back. They had accomplished their object, the possession of the train, and showed no disposition to molest the remainder of the party, but turned their attention to plundering the train and securing the stock. "This alone seemed to be the cause of the escape of these people, for the Indians did not attempt to follow them."[10]

The two young men on foot in the vanguard, Jacob and Joseph Reith, had left the wagon train at the moment of its being abandoned. They had seen Mr. and Mrs. Utter and their eldest daughter felled by the Indians as the train was overrun. The Reith brothers hustled off down the trail on foot. They hoped to try and overtake the mounted ex-dragoons.[11] Emeline recalled: "In the horrible tumult of the night we did not see them go, and did not know but they were killed."

The other twenty-seven fleeing emigrants got together as much as possible and made for the river as they were very thirsty. They had very little water through the fight.

> The wagons had been set on fire and the cattle driven out. It was at this time that the thought of trying to get away came to some one in the party, and crouching down and taking advantage of the darkness and every bunch of sage and rock, they travelled on in the direction in which they hoped to find water, leaving the beaten track. Walking as rapidly as those little feet were able, they went on, and sure enough they came to a small stream of water.[MM]

After they got a drink of water they rested a little, if it could be called resting. They had the awful fear in their minds that they would be followed and killed. They decided upon a course of action. They would keep away from the road, travel in single file, and as near as possible cover the tracks by having a man step in each track.[E]

> After resting a short time [they] went on, but, oh, so weary and hungry. A boy of eleven or twelve, as he left the wagon, seeing his two sisters in the group, grabbed a couple of corn cakes baked in a pie tin and

about one and one-half inches thick. This food was divided among all, and with a drink of water, they went on, expecting momentarily to hear the Indians yelling after them.[MM]

As the remainder of the Van Ornum party, Mr. Chase and his family, the Myers, and the survivors of the Utter family (Charles, Henry, Susan, and the three Trimble children) fled along the river, they could see fires behind them. They supposed the fires were from the wagons burning and the goods that could not be carried away. The Indians were too busy with their booty to follow them. The Indian women made their appearance at the scene of the massacre, and sagebrush fires were kindled so the Indians could better see their plunder. So, the families went on as fast as they could, traveling all night until about daylight.[12]

FOUR

Fleeing The Indians

The families of the Utter party traveled only a short distance that night. Just before daylight they hid in a thick clump of willows, camping quietly under the bank of the Snake River. No one spoke except in a whisper, fearing a listening Indian. At early dawn the Indians released the livestock which, guarded by Indian riders, made a rush for the river and water. Seeing their valued animals in the hands of the Snakes only added to the families' anguish. They laid concealed in the willows by the river all day as they thought it unsafe to travel. For Emeline Trimble, words could not describe her "agony as I looked on the faces of my little brothers and sisters, poor orphans now, and heard them cry piteously for father and mother, and if possible worse yet, crying for bread when I had none to give them."[E] The only provisions from the wagons was one loaf of bread, secured by Mr. Chase. Some of them had some fishhooks in their pockets, and the ladies made lines with the spool-thread which they had. They caught a few fish.

The Indians frequently rode to the river for water, but hurriedly returned to the wagons. They were so engrossed with their plunder that they seemed uninterested in the emigrants who had escaped. The Indians gorged themselves on the food from the wagons and reduced to ashes all of the goods they did not want or could not carry.

Later in the day, about mid-morning, the emigrants observed the Snakes going past, driving off some of the cattle. The Indians had divided their spoils and seemed to have split into small bands, going different ways. One band driving stock away passed within a few hundred yards of where the emigrants were hiding. While the Indians were passing, Susan Utter became frightened by the scared faces around her and commenced crying. With an aching heart, Emeline Trimble had to hold her hand over the mouth of her baby sister to stifle the cries.

An Indian mounted on the back of the black stallion led quite a procession of Indian ponies, captured horses, placid oxen, cows and their calves. The emigrant livestock being driven away were still guarded by the herd-dogs from the train. Many of the animals still had arrows embedded in their sides and backs, and the feathered shafts waved back and forth with every motion of the wounded animals. The Indians were decked out in various articles of clothing plundered from the train. Isabella Myers saw

'Pet', our favorite cow, going by, lowing as if in pain. I peeked through the willows and saw an arrow sticking in her side. Mother made signs for us to keep still as death, or the Indians would find us. Not a child moved until the Indians had passed.

Some of the Snakes had followed the emigrants' trail. The families observed the Indians watching them and noted the signal fires that were lighted. Just about dark of that day, 11 September, three Indians went past, shooting off their guns and whooping and yelling. With the Indians howling about their camp, the families laid very quiet until after dark. They then got up and traveled as fast as possible. All on foot, they followed the river downstream.* When tired out they would lie down and sleep a short time, then get up and travel along. They laid by in the day time, hiding among the willows that grew along the river, and traveled at night. They were still well armed, and an Indian dared not show his head. The Indians would not attack in the night, and were afraid to come about the emigrants in the daytime.[1]

---

*The South Alternate Trail could not follow the Snake River from Castle Butte, but cut across the hills to Sinker Creek and Sinker Creek Butte, and then began following the Snake River at Guffey Butte. The survivors of the Utter Massacre followed along the Snake, which undoubtedly had a footpath. The course they took along the river lies entirely within the present-day Snake River Birds of Prey Natural Area and past Swan Falls.

On the second night of travel, Samuel Gleason, the young man carrying Margaret's

> baby sister, came to mother saying, "Mrs. Myers, I am afraid you must take the baby, I can go no farther. Go on and leave me." On taking the baby, although it was very dark that night, mother felt her clothes were wet and sticky with blood. He had been wounded in his breast and said nothing until so weak from loss of blood and lack of food he could go no farther. Of course they would not hear of leaving him, but stopped to rest and dressed his wound, which was not very bad and only needed attention. A man named Van Orman had a small pocket flask with a little liquor, which I think he had been hiding, but was kind enough to produce. He was soon able to go on with the others, and got all right.

Emeline Trimble described the difficulty of traveling at night.

> One night brother Christopher was missing when we camped. You will remember that we traveled by moonlight and starlight, and we could not guess what had become of him, and one of the men went back and found that he had taken the road and gone on, instead of turning out where we did to camp. He found his tracks, but we did not see him until the next day, when we met him coming back to us.

The fleeing emigrants got so hungry during the third night's travel that they killed one of the two dogs which had followed them from the train. It was the Utter's faithful family dog that had shared their hardships through all the long journey. They built a small fire. The men cut willow twigs, sharpened them, and on the pointed sticks roasted and ate the dog. The portions did not amount to much, though, when the meat was divided among the group.

The families were followed for four days by a small band of Indians. It was supposed the Snakes tracked them all day, as they would come onto the families about the same hour each night. The Indians would not come within gunshot range, but kept yelling and whooping. It seemed as though they meant to haunt the emigrants all the time.

The fourth night, 13 September, the Indians did not come until later. The families had camped under a hill on a creek. Above them were rocks. While the emigrants hid among the willows under the overhanging rock, the Indians went up above and started rocks down. They were trying to roll the rocks onto the emigrants. The rocks, some almost as large as a chair, rolled into the creek, splashing those in hiding with water. Although the boulders came close, the families crouched against the high bank of the steep hill and the rocks did not strike them.

As the Indians did not seem anxious to attack the emigrants, Joseph Myers figured that they were just trying to force the families into the open, to see how many there were. Still, the families were given quite a scare. Mrs. Myers gagged her "baby with the corner of her apron until she was black in the face she was so afraid she would cry out or make some noise. All the others were too frightened to make a noise."MM

The families started off as soon as it was dark enough for them to travel with safety. They kept on all night, feeling sure that they would be safer elsewhere. The Indians must have finally given up the chase, as after the fourth day the emigrants did not see or hear anything to alarm them. The Indians did not trouble the families after that. Since the survivors now were able to travel unmolested, they began traveling by day and camping at night.[2]

]   Travel Along The Trail   [

Traveling was not easy for the emigrant families. There were eighteen children under sixteen years of age. Mark Van Ornum was only sixteen or seventeen. Then there were the three sets of parents plus old Mr. Goodsel Munson and the young man, Samuel Gleason. Carrie Myers, almost a year old, was often carried by Mrs. Myers, until she almost gave out. Joseph Myers carried the next of their youngest, the lame Harriet. The other Myers children had to walk. The Chases had to carry two-year-old Mary. Emeline Trimble carried and cared for her little sister, Susan Utter. They traveled in this way some eight or nine days. They made over seventy miles before they became too tired and weak from hunger to continue carrying the children.

The emigrant families had almost nothing to eat. A few days after eating the Utter's dog, they also killed Mr. Van Ornum's. They roasted and ate some of the meat, and carried the rest for future use. They caught fish in the streams when they could, sometimes with pretty good luck, some days not any. They would eat rosebuds and berries when they could get them. They ate the roots of peppermint dug from the mud beside the Snake river. "When the dogs were all eaten, father, while crawling through the sagebrush, ran across a rattlesnake, which he grabbed and killed, and which we ate."ᴹ

The men had become so weak from hunger that they could hardly stand. When divided among the group, the dog meat had not amounted to much even though every scrap was eaten. The children, too, were past going on. Although the days were quite warm, the nights were cold. They needed a shelter to sleep under.

The survivors had rounded the big bend of the Snake, where the river makes its turn to flow to the north for some three hundred miles. Just south of where Adrian, Oregon now stands, the river pushes in close to the high bluffs to the west. It was here that a lone cow came moseying along which had been left by some previous wagon train.

The families figured the cow had strayed away from the train ahead of them and was trying to go back home. Joseph Myers called the cow and she came to them. Although she was a very poor looking critter, the hungry emigrants shot her. (This was the first shot which had been fired since they had left the wagons.) They soon had a fire going and roasted the tough, stringy flesh. They carried the meat with them the next day to the Owyhee River. They ate as much of the cow as they could. They even charred the bones in the fire, enough so that they could be chewed. By mixing the cow's flesh with purslane and rose-berries, the emigrant families made the meat last for two weeks.[3]

]   Munson and Christy Go Ahead   [

The Reith brothers, on foot, had caught up with the mounted ex-soldiers the second day after the wagons had been abandoned. They had then traveled on together, following the trail to the west. They hoped to catch up with another wagon train or to reach some settlement or source of relief. At the crossing of the Malheur River (Vale, Oregon) the trail seemingly forked, one fork (the Oregon Trail) running more to the north toward the Snake River. The party of ex-soldiers and the Reith boys took the fork running up Malheur River and followed that road six days.* When they struck the foot of the Blue Mountains, where the road they were following was lost, it became evident that it was only an old abandoned road.[4]

The youngest of the ex-soldiers and the Reith brothers "tried to persuade the others to return to the main road, but were met with threats of death to any who would turn back or leave the party."[6] During the night the three quietly withdrew. They slipped away with the Van Ornum horse that young Chaffee was riding, and returned east, down the Malheur. Five days later (about 22 September) the Reiths, with the young dragoon deserter, were just returning to the main trail, where it crosses the Malheur, when they met Goodsel Munson and Christopher Trimble.[7]

---

*The U S Army's wagon road expeditions (with wagons) had looked for a route along the Malheur this and the previous summer, so there were recent tracks The old abandoned road that they followed were the tracks made by the Captain Elijah White party in the large emigration of 1845. Stephen H. L. Meek, the brother of Joe Meek, was the guide of the wagon train which fifteen years earlier tried a new way to the Willamette Valley, to bypass "the dread Blue Mountains." With 150 to 200 wagons, the White party met with disastrous results, losing more than 75 of the party; 400 survivors were finally rescued and taken to the Dalles. This was one of the worst journeys to the Oregon country. (See Footnote 5.)

The families had met the "poor emigrant cow" about six miles before reaching the Owyhee River. It was then, about 17 September, that Goodsel Munson and Christopher Trimble (almost eleven) were sent forward as an express. It was hoped that the two could reach the settlements and send back help. Christy Trimble and Mr. Munson had followed the trail and soon were traveling the main route of the Oregon Trail. The two had traveled some twenty-five miles when they reached the hot springs at the Malheur River crossing. It was there that they came upon Jacob and Joseph Reith.[ME]

Mr. Munson and Christy told the Reith brothers that they had traveled with the main party up to five days previously. At that time, they had left the families in a destitute condition, but the escaped emigrants had reached the Owyhee. They expected the families would reach the Malheur in a few days. Chaffee still had the horse and when he and the Reith brothers heard that the families were starving, they killed the horse and roasted the flesh. They sent back Christopher Trimble to inform the families of the men having gone forward for relief. Christopher was started back with all the horse meat he could carry. Poor Christopher, knowing how great the families' need, loaded himself so heavy that later he had to throw pieces away; the meat became so heavy that he could not carry all of it the nineteen miles to where he found the families.

The Reith brothers, Chaffee, and Munson kept some of the horse flesh for food. They went on, traveling afoot with all speed to try and reach Fort Walla Walla and send help to the families. The four pushed on to Burnt River where Chaffee and Munson gave out. Since they found a few salmon in the stream that were easily caught, Munson and Chaffee decided to remain there to fish until the main party should arrive. The Reith brothers continued ahead, pushing on toward the settlements.

Owyhee River
Looking upstream to railroad bridge. Emigrant crossing and Utter survivors' shelters were further upstream.

FIVE

Owyhee Camp

It was about 18 September* that the emigrant families were entirely exhausted and stopped traveling. They figured they had traveled some ninety to a hundred miles from where their wagon train had been overrun by the Indians, although it was just under seventy-five miles by the road. When they stopped traveling they were then on the Owyhee River, about three miles from the old deserted post of Fort Boise. This was near where the main trail again crossed the Snake River and made a juncture with the South Alternate Trail.[1] Emeline described their condition:

So far all were alive, although our sufferings were terrible, both from hunger and exposure. It was getting cold weather and we were without extra clothing nights, and commenced to suffer from the cold. Our shoes were worn off, and we were barefoot, or nearly so, and nights we would bury our poor bruised feet in the sand to keep them warm. We set to work and built us camps out of the boughs and brush which we could find along the river, for we could see little probability of getting away from here, and tried to make things as comfortable as possible.

Mr. (Joseph) Myers had escaped so far with his whole family, and had it not been for him I think we should have traveled along a little way each day

---

*From later interviews with Joseph Myers it was reported that it was about 17 September when they stopped traveling and that they "traveled in this way some eight or nine days." Since it was also reported that they were first attacked on the 8th instead of the 9th, the date of the 17th is incorrect.

Shelter 1	Shelter 2
Mr. Alexis Van Ornum	Mr. Joseph Myers
Mrs. Abagail Van Ornum	Mrs. Mary E. Myers
Marcus Van Ornum 'Mark'	Isabella Myers
Eliza Van Ornum	Margaret Myers 'Maggie'
Minerva Van Ornum	Eugene Myers
Reuben Van Ornum	Harriet Myers 'Hattie'
Lucinda Van Ornum	Carolyn Myers 'Carrie'
Samuel Gleason	Mr. Daniel Chase, Sr.
Charles Utter	Mrs. Elizabeth Chase
Henry Utter	Daniel Chase, Jr.
Emeline Trimble	Albert Chase
Elizabeth Trimble 'Libbie'	Mary Chase
Susan Utter	
Christopher Trimble 'Christy'	

Survivors at Owyhee Camp.   (Complied by Author).

toward the Fort [Walla Walla], which was to us a haven of safety, but he begged us piteously for us not to leave him, as he was not able to travel, that we would not go without him.

Some of the men who smoked had a few matches in their pockets when they fled the wagon train. At least they would have a fire while waiting for rescue.

The families made their camp on the Owyhee about 500 feet upstream from the road crossing.[2] The Owyhee was but a little, shallow river at that time of year. They built two rude shelters in the ground and, using their pocket knives, covered them with willows and grass. As they had no blankets and but little clothing, they piled a lot of grass inside and would crawl into their hut at night. The seven Myers and five Chases were in one shelter. The Van Ornum family, Samuel Gleason,

Charles and Henry Utter, Emeline and Elizabeth Trimble, and little Susan Utter shared the other; when Christopher Trimble rejoined his siblings, there were fourteen in this shelter.

Although the beef was made to last two weeks, by mixing it with "purslane and rose-berries" (another quote said "rose-buds and parsley"), it was not enough. The families ate snakes, lizards, frogs, and mussels out of the streams. Sometimes they could shoot ducks and geese.

Some Shoshoni tribes spent the early summer in the Boise Valley, trading, dancing, gambling and merrymaking as they harvested the fish and grains and other food items. They came mainly for the annual salmon run and dried the fish for a winter supply of food. Throughout the year, though, there always seemed to be some Indians encamped to fish on the Snake River and the mouth of the Boise, near the abandoned Hudson Bay Company fort. This was some three miles from where the emigrants were camping on the Owyhee River. It was about 1 October, almost two weeks after stopping on the Owyhee that the families were discovered by these Snake Indians.

> When we had been in camp some time, my brother Christopher was down by the river fishing one day, when an Indian came to him and seemed much surprised at seeing him, and wanted him to go home to his camp with him, but Christy told him that he had a camp of his own and must go to that. He went away, and Christy came home and told us. In about an hour the same Indian came back and had four more with him, and brought us one fish, but when they saw how many there were of us they went back and brought some more fish for us, and urged us to go to their camp with them but we would not go. We had a great horror of being taken captive by them. We traded some clothes with them for fish.[E]

The Indians called themselves 'Shoshones'. They seemed rather puzzled and wondering over the situation and condition they found the families in. Although the Indians seemed

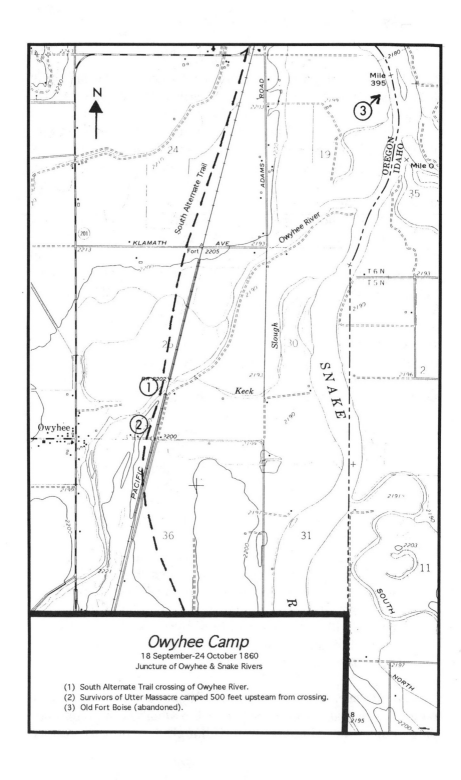

Owyhee Camp
18 September-24 October 1860
Juncture of Owyhee & Snake Rivers

(1) South Alternate Trail crossing of Owyhee River.
(2) Survivors of Utter Massacre camped 500 feet upsteam from crossing.
(3) Old Fort Boise (abandoned).

friendly and showed no inclination to harm them, still, the emigrants thought some of the Indians engaged in the massacre were among these Snakes. The Indians had brought salmon and wanted to "swap," a word that nearly all the Indians of the area used. The families exchanged some of their clothing and ammunition for the salmon. This was the only way they could obtain the food.

In a small chamois bag which she wore around her neck for fear of losing it, which she had worn since leaving the old home, [Margaret's] mother had several rings and a couple of brooches. She also carried in her pocket a few pins and needles, so frequently needed where there were so many children. These the Indians would take in exchange for their fish, also our dresses, my sisters and mine. My little brother's coat trimmed with bright buttons, mother's apron, and everything we could spare and remain covered, were all given to them at separate times. I could not say certainly how many times they came, I think three or four. Father had in his pocket about thirty dollars in silver coin, but this they did not want and would not give anything for it.[MM]

After the emigrants had sold most everything, the Indians refused to bring any more salmon unless the men would give them the guns. This the men did not wish to do. The Indians seemed quite determined to have the guns. Joseph Myers prudently buried his revolver and some ammunition.

The Indians took a dislike to the Van Ornum children as they were so hungry that they snatched the fish from the Indians and ate it greedily. The Shoshoni wanted Christopher Trimble to go home with them though. They indicated by signs that they would treat Christopher well and give him food.

Christopher volunteered to go home with the Indians, to stay with them in their camp, some three miles distant across the Snake river. Thus, he would do what he could to induce the Shoshoni to bring provisions to the families. Christopher begged his sister Emeline to let him go. He said that he was afraid that if none of the emigrants went, the Indians would not like it, and might harm the families. He said that if the Indians did not let him come back he could run away the next summer, get in with some emigrant train, and rejoin the others if they ever got through (which looked very doubtful). The Indians left, taking Christopher with them; they said that in three days they would be back, bringing the boy with them.

The Shoshoni treated Christopher Trimble kindly; they fed him and gave him a place to sleep. At the end of three days the Indians came back as they had agreed to, and they brought Christopher with them. They also brought fish. The Indians sold the salmon for any little items the emigrants could spare— such as needles, pins, and the rags on their backs. They traded in this way until the families were reduced virtually to a state of nakedness.

> One day they came bringing more fish than usual, and the women parted with everything they had to spare to get as much of it as possible. My [Margaret's] mother was now wearing just her skirt and underwear, having exchanged her dress for food. The rest of the women and the children being very scantily clad. My father tried to trade his hat, but the Indians only patted his head and put it back on him. For some unaccountable reason they did not want it, as all the Indians we saw were hatless. I suppose they thought headgear was a nuisance, as they even spared me my sunbonnet which my dear grandmother gave me the morning we started.[MM]

Joseph Myers may have had some influence on the Indians. This might have been due to his bright, red hair, which showed through the holes of his bullet-riddled hat. The Indians were quite curious.[3]

The Shoshoni had brought more dried salmon to trade than previously; they wanted the guns. At length they became insolent. Without leave they carried off four guns: two from

Mr. Van Ornum, one from Mr. Chase, and one from Myers.
They also took Mr. Van Ornum's blanket from him, and they
did it somewhat roughly. In return for the guns, the Indians
gave what salmon they pleased, and promised more (which
they did not bring).

]   Van Ornum Party Leaves   [

After the Indians left, Mr. Van Ornum said he was going
to take his portion of fish and his family and leave; "For," he
said, "if we do not, the Indians will come tomorrow and strip
and kill us."ᴹ The families talked it over and agreed that when
this band of Indians did come back that they might kill them.

Joseph Myers tried to persuade Van Ornum not to go by
pointing out that they were as well off where they were as they
would be wasting what little strength they had left in traveling.
Alexis Van Ornum resolved to leave as they could buy no more
food on the Owyhee. He, his wife, and five children would
travel on as well as they could and maybe they would find food
or help. Mrs. Van Ornum did not want to go, but they got together what provisions they could, dividing everything fairly
with the others, even to the few matches that were left.

As the Van Ornum family prepared to start, Charles Utter
begged to go with them. So too did Henry Utter. Samuel
Gleason was also determined to leave the camp.[4] They refused, however, to allow Emeline Trimble to go with them.
The Van Ornum party left camp that day about noon, heading
out along the trail to try and reach Fort Walla Walla.

Mr. Chase, being so starved, ate too hearty a meal on the
salmon brought by the Indians that day. He ate so much of it
that he was thrown into the hiccoughs. He died sometime during the night, probably from over-eating the salmon. He was
buried the next day in a shallow grave that Joseph Myers dug
beside the Owyhee River. "The little party was now more
lonely, hopeless and sad than ever, as it consisted of only ten
persons, Chrissie still being with the Indians."ᴹᴹ

After staying with the Indians a few more days, Christopher Trimble returned again with them to the Owyhee camp. They brought salmon and traded with the remaining emigrants. While Christopher was there, Joseph Myers inquired of him how far it was to the Shoshoni's camp. He answered, about three miles. Myers then asked him how far it was after crossing the river before the path to the Indian camp was struck. Chris said just a short distance and the trail was plain. He inquired of Myers why he was asked this? Myers told him, if the soldiers came to their relief they would want to come for him. The word "soldier" was frequently used by the emigrants in relation to expected help.[M]

The Indians at once seemed to understand the word, "soldier," as it excited their curiosity. They straightened up and murmured "soja, soja, soja." The word passed from one to the other and a curious, devilish look seemed to pervade their countenances. They talked among themselves and soon left the emigrant camp. Christopher followed after the Indians, saying they were kind to him and gave him plenty of food. It was arranged that he should be sent for as soon as any help arrived, and that he should return with the Indians in another three days to visit. They never returned; not an Indian after that made an appearance.[M] Emeline did not see her brother this time as she was away from the camp gathering fuel for the fire.

> I came back with my fuel, and when on my way out quite aways from camp I heard a frightful noise. It seemed to me more like dogs fighting than anything else I heard. I was scared, and made haste into camp, and they told me Christy had been there and gone back again. We waited with as much anxiety as we could feel about anything until the three days were passed and the Indians did not come back and we felt afraid of them, and we began to talk about trying to start along, but I could not go without finding something of the fate of Christy.

The party at the camp subsisted almost two more weeks, mostly on herbs, frogs, and mussels which they gathered or caught and ate. These were found in great scarcity along the river. They had no fishing tackle. They would eat rosebuds, berries, snakes, and lizards when they could get them. If the Indians had not robbed them of their guns, Joseph Myers thought they "could have made a living by killing game, which was tolerably plenty" where they camped on Owyhee River.^M

After the Van Ornums left, those left at the Owyhee camp (starving and suffering with cold) were hoping that the others had escaped and would send or bring help. They huddled over their tiny fire of dried dung and sagebrush; they were almost too weak to go out and gather fuel. They did not dare allow the fire to go out as they had only a few matches left.

The emigrants left in the Owyhee camp kept alive by hunting anything they possibly could. When they did find a piece of a carcass, they made use of it. They were getting so weak that they could scarcely walk about. They ate moss, weeds, grass, and anything at all they could find. Starvation was staring them in the face.

They found a patch of some variety of thick leaved moss, about twenty-five feet long and a few feet wide, which in their starving condition they were brave enough to eat. For several days they pulled and ate it raw. Never was anything cherished or used so carefully. Not one stem or leaf was trampled or wasted, but it created a gas in the stomachs if eaten too freely. Then one day one of the party, wandering aimlessly around, found, a mile or more away, a flat piece of rusty sheet iron, and lying on the sand, some staves, and underneath, perhaps a double handful of rock salt, rusty, dirty, but oh, how welcome.

I [Margaret] well remember how joyfully they came in displaying their treasure, and the disappointment of the children who could see nothing in that to eat. Using a rock taken from the stream, they succeeded in hammering it into a small square pan that held water. Now they could cook their moss, and best of all, a few grains of the precious salt made it more palatable and digestable [*sic*]. Soon the moss was gone and did not spring up again. I forgot to say they found a few empty fresh water mussel shells. These they used for spoons. Seated in a circle each one had one dip, alternately, children getting as much as adults. Sometimes my parents would give their spoonful to one or another of the children, themselves doing with less. So it was with everything they had after the moss was gone.[MM]

Mrs. Myers said "she would dream of making large loaves of bread—dream a great deal about piles and piles of something to eat."[M] Mrs. Chase had the misfortune to lose the use of one limb and the arm on the same side, and was almost entirely helpless for a part of the time they were in the Owyhee camp.[E] Mrs. Myers

remonstrated with Mrs. Chase for eating and not giving the food to her children. Mrs. Chase said, "I don't feel that I can kill my children, but I want them to die, for fear I should die first and they might fall into the hands of the Indians."[IM]

Joseph Myers thought that Mrs. Chase was too selfish, that

she lived too well herself and starved her child. She would scold my wife because we gave our children so much; she argued that we were all bound to die right there, and that it was better that the children should die first, than for us to die, and leave our children to the mercy of the wolves—but my wife said she believed that Providence would yet deliver us, and that we should all try to keep alive as long as possible.[M]

Emeline Trimble had some critical comments too.

The hardship of gathering fuel and subsistence was not shared by Mr. Myers' family. He said they were not able. Even the task of washing for their baby was allotted to me, and often when we would go out after pusley, rosebuds, and such other vegetation as we could find which we could eat, and leave Mr. Myers praying, I suppose in a selfish way for his own family, in camp instead of helping in our hardships, on our return the other children would cry and beg for something to eat and say the Myers family had been eating fish, or whatever we had stored away for rations, for we had to allow each one just so much at a meal.

Margaret explained that her Mother was

a praying woman and had always said God would deliver us out of this trouble. Many times in after years I heard her say when telling this story to people, and they would ask her how it happened all her children were saved and others were taken, hinting perhaps we had been favored with more food, she would tell them we were saved by her prayers. She and father were the only believers, the others scoffed and railed at the idea of God's care.

Emeline described the plight of her

poor sister Libbie, nine years old, used to help me gather buffalo chips for fuel, and rosebuds, pusley [purslane] and other things to eat. She and I went to gather fuel as usual one morning, and she was tugging along with all she could carry and she fell behind. I carried mine into camp and went back to meet her; I called her name and she made no answer. Soon I found her, and I said, "Libbie, why did you not answer?" She said, "I could not talk I felt too bad," and before night she was dead.

It was some ten days after Mr. Chase died that Elizabeth Trimble also died, from starvation. Four or five days afterwards her little sister, Susan Utter, died. The next day eight-year-old Daniel Chase, Jr. died, and two days after him his younger brother, Albert. The children all died from the same terrible cause, starvation.[M]

After much hesitation, those who remained alive resolved to eat the bodies of the dead, with the hope of preserving their own lives until relief should come. It was a subject of much anxious consultation, and even of prayer, before the decision finally was taken to eat the dead. This determination was unanimous. The bodies of the four children were thus disposed of, no more being used than was absolutely necessary for subsistence. The flesh of the dead was carefully husbanded and sparingly eaten to make it go as far as possible. Mrs. Chase "helped eat her own children."[M] The traumatic effects of this dire situation was aptly summarized by Emeline:

> Starvation was making sad inroads on our little band, and none but those who have endured the awful pangs of starvation can have even a faint idea of such horrible sufferings and death. We became almost frantic, food we must have, but how should we get it? Then an idea took possession of our minds which we could not even mention to each other, so horrid and revolting to even think of, but the awful madness of hunger was upon us, and we took and ate the bodies of each of the poor children, first sister Libbie, then Mr. Chase's little boys, and next my darling little baby sister whom I had carried in my arms through all the long dreary journey and slept with hugged to my heart as though if possible I would shield her from all danger. She too had to leave me. In vain had I saved the choicest morsel of everything for her, chewed fish and fed it to her, boiled pusley [sic] which we found on the Snake River and fed her the water and everything which I could plan had been fed to keep her alive. Mrs. Myers and Mrs. Chase each had babies about her

age, but neither could spare a share of nature's own food for our poor little motherless one, for fear of robbing her own. For forty days I carried her, but had to give up at last, and I was left alone. All who had depended on me had been taken except the two step brothers who had gone on and from whom we had heard nothing.

]   Search For Christopher   [

The people at the camp on the Owyhee waited in vain for word from Christopher Trimble. After nearly two weeks, without seeing either he or the Shoshoni, Emeline went to the Snake River. She could see the Shoshoni camps but could not see any living thing around them. For some time she called loudly for her brother without seeing him or getting any response; just the echo of her own voice was all the answer she could hear. She went back to camp feeling sure something had happened to the boy.

The next day Mrs. Chase and Mr. Myers went to the river to find the Indians and trade for more salmon. They could not find them. The Indians had been camped some three miles below the emigrants, across the Snake river. The following day Mr. Myers went again, alone, opposite the place and saw a few wigwams, but no sign of any Indians. He fired several shots across the river towards their camp and "hallooed" loudly. He hoped this would bring young Trimble or the Indians across the Snake, but he could not obtain any answer. He concluded that they had gone.

On the way back to his camp, Myers saw where the 'wolves' had dragged something across the path which went from his camp to that of the Shoshoni. He followed up the trace, hoping it might be where some animal had dragged along the carcass of a deer, and that he might find a piece to take home. He followed the track a short distance and found two locks of human hair, which resembled Christopher Trimble's. He took the fragments to camp and Emeline recognized it as her brother's.

Then he knew that my brother had been killed by the Indians, and his body torn to pieces by the wolves. He came back to camp and told us, and words cannot describe my feelings as I heard of his horrible fate. I knew then that the noise which I heard that day was my poor brave Christy whom I loved so well. I thought I had passed through all the suffering which I could endure, and God knows how I longed to lie down and die and be at rest, but it was not to be so, nor had I drained the cup to the dregs yet.

Also on his way home that day, Mr. Myers found the carcass of a horse that he thought the 'wolves' had deserted. Those coyotes had left but little meat on it. He picked up a shank and took it to camp. The emigrants used that whole carcass; they burnt the bones and ate them and roasted the skins.

Some Indians must have come along, as one day they dug up Mr. Chase's body, took the few rags of clothing it had on, and buried him again. Later, the starving emigrants made up their minds to try and eat Mr. Chase's remains. The body had been buried over ten days. So, on 24 October, they exhumed the body, cut it into small pieces, a day's ration in a piece. Just as the first meal from it was roasted and about to be eaten, Margaret's

mother had gone away to pray, Emmaline was wandering in search of buffalo chips for the fire, and hoping to find along the river bank a few rose buds. They had found a few one day and eaten them. Mother's mouth was very sore at this time from eating them. She had returned to camp when we saw Emmaline running, or trying to, falling, staggering to her feet and trying to run on. They thought she was crazed, but when she got where they could hear, she cried out someone was coming. All got to their feet, fearing Indians, but by this time they had seen her and were riding fast.

SIX

News Of The Massacre

The three discharged soldiers, who attempted to cross the Blue Mountains high up the Malheur, were attacked by Indians on what was thought to be the headwaters of the John Day River. Two were killed but ex-private Henry Snyder became the first of the Utter Party to reach help. He made it out of the Blue Mountains the end of September and was found by some teamsters who were in the service of the Indian Department. On the night of the 30th he was brought into the camp of George E. Cole* on Willow Creek.[1]

Snyder had reached help at a critical moment, as starvation and thirst were fast doing their work. He was so completely exhausted and worn down that it was with great difficulty that he could tell even a part of his story. He "felt sure that every member of his party but himself had been killed by the Indians."[2] The next morning, Monday, 1 October, Cole sent Thomas Burke with a letter to The Dalles with news of the massacre. Burke also had heard Snyder tell his story.

It was two or three days before Snyder could make any report. His story was very contradictory, and did not agree with the facts as afterward developed. At the end of the week Snyder made it to The Dalles.[3] He "told so many lies on getting to the fort that they did not believe that there was any train in trouble."[E]

---

*George Edward Cole was 33 at this time. He came to Oregon in 1850; had been a member of the Oregon Legislature, 1852-53; was Postmaster at Corvallis in 1858; was a clerk of U S courts for District of Oregon, 1859-60; and this year moved to Walla Walla, W. T. Later he steamboated on the Upper Columbia in 1861; was elected to the 38th Congress, 1863-65; was appointed governor of Washington Territory by President Johnson in November 1866 and served until 4 March 1867; returned to Oregon and engaged in railroad construction; was appointed Postmaster of Portland in 1873 and served until 1881; moved back to Washington and was elected treasurer of Spokane County; died in Portland 3 Dec 1906. (See Endnote 4.)

Area newspapers soon reported Snyder's tale, further confusing his inaccurate account. The *North-West* of Port Townsend, W. T., on 11 October 1860 copied two articles that were printed in the *Portland Advertiser* on the 4th:

SHOCKING MURDER OF FORTY-FIVE
EMIGRANTS BY THE SNAKE INDIANS.

By the *Julia* last evening we received a letter from our Dalles correspondent, who informs us that news had reached that place to the effect that forty-five emigrants had been butchered in cold blood by the Snake Indians. The massacre took place on Salmon river, [*sic*] about 175 miles from the Dalles. The train comprised forty-six persons, including women and children, all of whom, with the exception of Mr. Shrieder, were brutally murdered. The Indians entered the encampment of the emigrants, and while the latter were not suspecting any treachery, instantaneously commenced a general onslaught upon the entire party. The men in the company resisted to their utmost, but finding that the Indians were likely to kill off the entire party if they stayed, six of them took to flight, but were shortly after overtaken by about ninety Indians, and five of them shot down. Upon the fall of his comrades, Mr. Shrieder, the only survivor of the train, immediately took to the brush, where he lived on berries for seven days before he met with some white citizens, to whom he told his sad tale, and by whom he was relieved.

We hope immediate steps will be taken to punish those marauding savages, who have thus ruthlessly murdered in cold blood a company of American emigrants.

After the foregoing was in type, the same paper received a letter from George E. Cole, a late resident of Portland, of which they publish the subjoined extract:[5]

Willow Creek, O., Oct. 1, 1860

The bearer will tell you of the recent massacres on Salmon river, [*sic*] below Salmon Falls. A party of emigrants from Illinois, consisting of eight wagons, with which there were nine discharged soldiers from Fort Hall, were attacked and all but six of the party killed.

Among the party were two men by the name of Myres. The soldiers spoken of were discharged dragoons, who charged through the Indians, and succeeded in making their escape, but lost their road, and were again attacked and all but one killed.

The survivor got into camp last night in a state bordering on starvation. He was seven days and nights reaching this place across the mountains; without food, except what few berries he could pick up. He will be in to the Dalles in a few days when you can get full particulars. I have talked with the man and place confidence in his tale.

GEO. E. COLE.

Cole's letter was also reprinted in the 6 October issue of the *Weekly Oregonian* and in the *Sacramento Daily Union* on the 11th. Two days before, the *Sacramento Bee* had run the following account which, via the Overland Express, also appeared in the *New York Times* on the 23d:[6]

TELEGRAPHIC

Forty-five Emigrants murdered by Indians.

YREKA, October 9, 1860—1 P.M.

The following is an extra from the Vancouver Chronicle: "Vancouver, Oct. 3d, 9, P.M.—H. Schreider had just arrived at the Dalles, with news of the massacre, by the Snake Indians, of an entire emigrant train, consisting of forty-six persons—nineteen of whom were men, and the balance women and children. The party were first attacked about fifty miles this side of Salmon Falls, on the 9th of September. This attack lasted about one hour, when the Indians withdrew, and allowed the train to proceed five miles, where they again attacked them. The fight lasted, with intermissions, two days and one night. On the afternoon of the 10th, the Indians had possession of the whole train, with the exception of six men, who being mounted, escaped, and after traveling through the woods for nine days, they were again attacked and five of the party killed—Schreiber alone escaping by hiding in the bushes, and after traveling several days without food was found in an exhausted condition by some persons who took him to the Dalles. Of the nineteen males in the party, six were discharged soldiers from Fort Hall. Mr. Schreiber is the only one who escaped, and says the six men who left on horseback did not leave until the Indians had complete possession of the train, and from the screams of the women and children, is led to believe that the whole party were butchered."

The *Pioneer and Democrat* of Olympia, W.T., on 12 October republished the following 8 October account from *The Dalles Mountaineer*:

ATTACK UPON AN EMIGRANT TRAIN

FORTY-FIVE PERSONS SLAIN BY INDIANS

Last week a report reached us that an emigrant train had been attacked by Snake Indians, and one man killed and another seriously wounded.* This occurred on the road between Salmon Falls and Fort Boise. Another, and a still more painful rumor reached us on Monday last, [1 October] through Thomas Burke, who tells the following, as he received it from Henry

---

*This was the wagon train thirteen days ahead of the Utter Party.

Snyder, at Willow Creek, some sixty-five miles from the Dalles:

Henry Snyder, a discharged soldier from Utah, with two comrades, joined an emigrant train which left Fort Hall under a Dragoon escort, and traveled with it to Snake River. When near Salmon Falls, the escort returned to Fort Hall, having accompanied the emigrants as far as the supply of rations would allow them to go. The emigrant party then numbered forty-six souls, including women and children. When they reached a point about twenty miles west of Salmon Falls, their oxen having been obliged to go for a day and a half without water, the train was directed towards the river in order to supply them. This was on the evening of Sept. 13th [*sic*]. Just as they reached the river bank, the Snake Indians appeared in large numbers upon the hills near and attacked them with arrows and rifles. A running fight ensued which lasted two days. The Snakes picked off the ox drivers occasionally until only four men, including Snyder, were left at the end of the second day. These four took each a good horse from some led horses that belonged to one of them, and ran for their lives. They took an old track, which was soon lost in the night, being overgrown with grass, after which they fled to the hills south of the river. They killed one horse for food, and took turns in walking. While Snyder was walking ahead, about the 17th of Sept., in the mountains, he heard shots fired, and saw his comrades fall from their horses. One of the loose horses ran forward and he caught it and galloped off, the Indians pursuing. The horse fell in a rocky ravine, in the evening, and Snyder ran to a creek and concealed himself in the bushes, losing his revolver as he fell. In the night he crept out, and after wandering in the hills seven days, during which time he subsisted on rosebuds and juniper berries, he was found by some teamsters who were in the service of the Indian

Department, and brought to Willow Creek. During
two days before he was found he had no water. He is
likely to recover, though very much worn down. The
above is all that could be gathered from him during the
time that Burke saw him. He was too much exhausted
to speak easily, and his voice, when he was found had
sunk to a mere whisper.

P. S. After the above was in type, Snyder arrived
at the Dalles, and fully confirmed the statement of
Burke. He still suffers much, and is under the care of
Dr. A. J. Hogg, with every prospect of speedy recovery.—*Mountaineer, Oct. 8.*[7]

]   Bureau of Indian Affairs and the Army   [

In addition to the Army being notified of the massacre, the
US Interior Department, through its Bureau of Indian Affairs,
was anxiously involved. On 4 October the Oregon Superin-
tendent of Indian Affairs, Edward R. Geary, quickly wrote to
Colonel George Wright (Department of Oregon commander) at
Fort Vancouver:

The melancholy intelligence, from sources entitled
to credit, has just reached this Office of the murder by
the Digger Snakes of a party of forty-five Immigrants
at a point below the Salmon Falls of Salmon River. A
Mr Shrieder, supposed to be the only survivor of the
Company, made his excape and after subsisting for
seven days on wild berries, succeeded in reaching the
camp of Mr Geo E. Cole on Willow Creek in an almost famished state on the night of the 30th ultimo.

This tragic event must have occurred soon after
Major Grier's command set out on their return, and is
another striking evidence of the stealthy and covert
movements of these savage marauders and murders.

Humanity, the obligation of the Government to the
citizen and the general prosperity of Oregon and

Washington, demand that prompt and vigorous measures be taken to inflict summary chastisement on these miscreants and for the future security of immigrants and the frontiers.

There is reason to believe that there are parties of immigrants still on the plains and exposed to danger. I have also serious apprehension for the safety, not only of the Warm Spring Reservation, but also of that on Wild Horse Creek, and of the settlements in that vicinity, and would most respectfully and earnestly press on your consideration the importance of so disposing of the military forces of the neighboring posts as to avert, if practicable further disasters to the lives and property of our citizens, and of the friendly Indians who have the solemn guaranty of treaties for their protection.

I enclose you a slip from the "Advertisor" of this morning, relating to the massacre.[8]

The same day Superintendent Geary also wrote to Commissioner A. B. Greenwood, his superior in Washington, DC. In this letter he correctly placed the Utter massacre on the Snake River instead of the Salmon. He also explained why there were no longer soldiers on the trail when the Utter train was attacked.

It is my painful duty to communicate to you, that reliable intelligence has reached this office of the massacre of a large company of immigrants near the Salmon Falls of Snake River by the Digger Snakes. The company consisted of forty-six persons—men women and children—enroute for Oregon, of who forty-five are supposed to have fallen victims to savage barbarity. Mr. Shreider alone escaped and after enduring the greatest privations and travelling day and night—for a whole week, succeeded in reaching the camp of Mr. Geo. E. Cole on Willow Creek about 100 miles East of the Dalles in Middle Oregon.

The command of Major Grier /2 companies of
Dragoons/ spent several weeks in the region where
this trajedy is alleged to have occurred without finding
the Indians anywhere in force or discovering evidence
of their being numerous in that vicinity. Supposing
the immigration to have generally, if not entirely, passed the region of peril, he returned with his command
to their quarters at Fort Walla Walla. Scarcely had his
return been accomplished, before the occurence of this
barbarous slaughter of our citizens, who after accomp-
lishing their long pilgrimage over the plains, were des-
tined to fall by the murderous hand of the relentless
savage, on the confines of the country of their destina-
ntion. I may here also state, that the command of Major Stein had only a few days returned to Fort Dalles
from his campaign into the Snake Country in the vicinity of Harney . . . Lake, before the aggressions of
these marauders were recommenced on the Warm
Spring Reservation, and forty horses, belonging to the
friendly Indians at that point, driven away. Apprehensions are now seriously entertained by Agent
Dennison, that an attack by a large body of these marauders is impending, and that unless military protection be speedily afforded, the reservation will be
desolated.

I have already communicated with Col Wright
commanding the Department, in regard to these frontier troubles, and have no doubt his experience and
energy will prompt him at the earliest moment practicable to make such a disposition of the forces as will
prevent further disaster and punish these miscreants.[9]

The Army's plans were followed in the press as reported
by the *Olympia Pioneer and Democrat:*

The Massacre

ARMY.—Much credit is due the gallant and energetic commander of the Military Department of

Oregon for the prompt and we hope effectual, measures he has taken to punish the Indians concerned in the late massacre, and to prevent the recurrence of a similar calamity. Col. Wright received the late melancholy intelligence on the 3d inst., and on the following day issued orders to Capt. F. Dent, 9th Inf., to proceed immediately with company E, a detachment of company I, 1st Dragoons, and forty enlisted men of companies B and E, 9th Inf., selected by himself, to the scene of the reported massacre, for the purpose of rescuing any survivors that may be found, from the hands of the Indians, and, if the opportunity offers, punishing the aggressors. The command will take rations for forty days, and other supplies will be furnished from Fort Walla Walla.

A detachment of I company, 1st Dragoons, is also ordered to proceed forthwith to the Warm Springs' reservation, in order to afford protection in case of attack by the Snake Indians, and to remain there until further orders.

Doubtless the Government will now see when it is too late, the necessity for the Military Post at Fort Boise; which has not even been commenced yet, although we have reason to believe an appropriation was made by Congress some time since for that purpose.

There are little grounds for believing that expeditions merely, will suffice to reduce these marauding savages and to keep them in subjection. Until that country is permanently occupied by the troops and every murderer properly punished, there can be no security from their continued outbreaks. The season is too far advanced to commence operations on a large scale: however, all that can possibly be done at present will no doubt be effected by Col. Wright and the troops under his command, and we hope that the present expedition will shortly be able to give a good account on its return.

The *Olympia Pioneer and Democrat* continued with this reprinted article from a source nearer Army headquarters, the *Vancouver Chronicle*:

Since the above was "set up," we have received further and more reliable advices from the scene of the late massacre in the Snake country, representing that affair in a much more favorable light than at first reported. From the last account we gather that but ten were killed by the Indians; six men, three women and one child.

It is believed that the man Schrieder who brought in the first account of the massacre, did not stop to count the number of killed, but left as fast as a good horse could carry him.

The remainder of the emigrants are making their way in, but slowly, as they have lost their train and animals.

The Indians having accomplished their object, the possession of the train, showed no disposition to molest the remainder of the party, but made off at once with their booty.

The hostile disposition of the Snake tribe, as shown in the events that have transpired in their country within the last few months, demonstrate the necessity of establishing Military Posts in that portion of Oregon. That this is a necessity well known to the war department, is evident from the fact, that last year orders were issued directing a fort to be established at or near Fort Boise, which would place a large portion of the emigrant road passing through the Snake country under the supervision of the troops.

The necessity for this fort is now more apparent than at the time that order was issued, and we hope the war department will issue the proper orders to that effect at once, and that they will be carried into immediate execution.

With Military stations in this country, one near the "camas ground," and one near the "fisheries," these Indians must, in a short time, be forced to submit or starve. Their mountain fastnessess will not then avail them in avoiding punishment for their misdeeds, the whole force of the Military can be promptly brought to bear on them, and they must sue for peace or be driven from their country.—*Vancouver Chronicle, Oct. 12.*[10]

The 'further and more reliable advices' mentioned above came from the Reith brothers. The two had finally reached assistance three weeks after the wagons were abandoned.

] Reith Brothers [

Joseph and Jacob Reith came in to the Umatilla Reservation on 2 October 1860. George H. Abbott* was the first Indian Agent for the newly established Umatilla Reservation. When the Reith brothers arrived at the Agency, he was at The Dalles, superintending the transportation of supplies to the agency. He had left in charge Byran N. Dawes, an employee of the agency.[11]   Abbott later recounted the Reith's story, wherein he had the two brothers confused:

While descending the western slope of the Blue mountains the two boys came to some cattle grazing on the hillside. They had a muzzle loading, double barreled shotgun with which they had been enabled to kill an occasional bird, and one of the boys was in favor of killing one of the cows, but the other objected on the ground that as they had been out of shot for some time and were using fine gravel instead of shot they would be unable to kill one; and further that where there were cattle there must be people close and if they were to

---

*He would turn thirty-one later in the month, was born in Ohio, and had come to Oregon in 1849 as a soldier in Loring's Mounted Rifles.

kill any of the cattle they would be considered thieves and be treated as such. So they pursued their way and in an hour or two saw a bunch of calves making their way through the brush and crossing the Umatilla river. Joe, who was the older and stronger, told his brother to remain quietly on the road while he would follow the calves, as he believed they would lead him to a white settlement, and promised to return for Jake as soon as possible. He therefore followed the calves through the brush along the river bottom out to the opening north of the river, where he found himself in the midst of an Indian village. As he was seen at once, he decided to trust the Indians instead of trying to escape, and as soon as he could do so made them understand that he wished them to take him to Walla Walla. The Indians were willing to do this, and catching a pony one of the Indians mounted and told Joe to get on behind, as he saw at a glance that the boy was not able to ride alone. But Joe then explained as best he could by words and signs that there was another to be taken. The Indians then made him understand that there was a white chief on the other side of the river and Joe, thinking that it must be an Indian agent, at once requested to be taken there. He was so weak, however, that the Indians, thinking he would fall off his horse, had another brave mount behind Joe to hold him on, and thus they crossed the river three on one horse. Jake had grown tired waiting for his brother, and moving slowly along the road soon came in sight of a building only about one hundred yards distant, and hastened to them, so that when Joe reached the agency he found Jake already there.

This was twenty-two days from the time they left the train on Snake river, eleven [?] days of that time having been wasted in the trip up Malheur river. The boys had lived on a few birds, part of the horse spoken of, a little salmon caught in Burnt river, and wild rose berries, snakes, frogs, and one rabbit. They were so exhausted, starved and wasted that their minds were as weak as their bodies, and it was difficult for them to tell a coherent story.[12]

As soon as Dawes could comprehend the conditions of the emigrants as reported by the Reith brothers, he acted. On the night of the Reiths' arrival, Dawes started two men—well mounted—with one pack mule loaded with provisions. He instructed the men to travel day and night until they met the emigrants. The next morning Dawes started another man with a yoke of oxen and a light wagon loaded with food and supplies for all, and in which to bring the exhausted survivors.[13]

Dawes had in the meantime reported to the military authorities at Fort Walla Walla such facts as he had been able to gather from the Reith brothers. He also had written a letter that was widely reprinted in the newspapers of Oregon, Washington Territory, and, a month later, the *New York Times*:

ANOTHER INDIAN MASSACRE—A correspondent of the Dalles *Mountaineer*, writing from the Umatilla Reservation under date of 3d inst., says:—On yesterday two brothers, named Keith, arrived here reporting that the train to which they belonged had been attacked by the "Shoshones," or Bannock tribe of Indians; that a large number of immigrants had been killed, and the remainder driven away from their wagons and scattered. The men arrived here much exhausted, subsisting on some dried horse meat for twenty-one days. The names of the murdered are as follows: J. Myers, Wm. Auttely, Lewis Lawson, Chas. Kersner, Elijah Otter, his wife, three daughter, and one son. When the brothers Keith left the train, there were alive, Jos. Myers, wife and five children, A. McNorman, wife and five children, Daniel Chase, wife and three children, Samuel Gleason, Chas. Jeffy, Mr. Munson, and six children of Elijah Otter. When last heard from they had nothing to eat. I have started some assorted provisions to their assistance, and sincerely hope it will

arrive in time to save them from starvation. The attack
was made between Salmon Falls and Ft. Boise. If yet
alive, my supplies will meet them on Burnt river or
Goose creek.[14]

Abbott arrived back at the Umatilla Agency on 4 October,
the day after the ox team had been started out to the relief of the
Utter party survivors. He immediately forwarded a supple-
mental report to the same military officers that Dawes had
informed. Also, he reported in full to the Superintendent of
Indian affairs for Oregon, at Portland, all the facts that had
reached the Agency and the Agency's action thereon.

The two men in advance with the pack mule pushed ahead,
watching carefully for sign of the emigrants. They struck
Burnt River and went down it, following the trail about forty
miles, to where later the railroad town of Huntington would
be. Here, the Burnt River turns east to empty into the Snake,
three miles further on. The Oregon Trail continues southeast
four miles, over high ground to hit the Snake at Farewell
Bend. The advance party went no farther; they had passed the
point at which Munson and Chaffee were left to fish without
having met anyone. They had found tracks of women and
children, some of whom wore shoes. The two men started on
their return thinking that the emigrants must have left the main
road and that the two had passed the emigrant party before going so far. While on the return trip the two men continued their
search for the families, and took great care in searching the
country. The advance party failed to find anyone and met
Copenhaver with the ox team in the Powder River Valley on
what was then called Powder River Slough. Unfortunately the
distressed travelers had remained on the Owyhee. The relief
party sent out by Dawes arrived back at the Umatilla Reservation about the 10th (the eighth day after being sent out), worn
out and discouraged, having traveled night and day, hoping to
see the fires lighted by the sufferers by night.

When the Dawes relief party returned, Agent Abbott "was
exceedingly sorry that I had not been at the agency when the
Reith brothers had arrived there, for the reason, that either

Dawes or myself would have gone with the advance party, and turned back for nothing until we had found the immigrants."[15]

George Abbott's superior in the Bureau of Indian Affairs gave direction to the Umatilla agent's endeavors and kept him abreast of relief efforts:

> Office Supt. Ind. Affairs
> Portland Ogn, Oct. 10th 1860

Sir:

As you are the Officer of the Indian Service most convenient to the Scene of the late massacre of a large party of Immigrants by the Snake Indians, which is said to have occurred about 90 miles west of the Salmon Falls, you are directed to use all proper efforts to ascertain whether any of the immigrants have escaped, and to use all required endeavors in such case to complete the rescue of such unfortunate persons and afford them aid.

I do not think it calculated to promote the object for you to accompany the expedition. You will however hold yourself in readiness to meet any emergency that may arise, and are authorized to act in the premises without awaiting further instructions from the Office.

Col. Wright informed me, that if at any time military aid may be required for the protection of the Umatilla Reservation, it may be readily summoned from the Post at Fort Walla Walla.

I am very respectfully

To　　　　　　　　　　}　　Your obt servant
　Geo H. Abbott Esq. }　　　Edward R. Geary
　　Sub Ind. Agent　}　　　Supt Ind Affairs
　　　Umatilla　　　}
　　　　Ogn　　　　}[16]

Farewell Bend

Farewell Bend and State Park to the right; Old US 30 follows route of Oregon Trail over hill to Huntington, Oregon.

SEVEN

Army Relief Expedition

While the people of the US Bureau of Indian Affairs were attempting to assist the survivors of the Utter massacre, the US Army was also in motion. As Abbott later wrote, the "commanding officer at Walla Walla had reported to the commanding officer for the District of Oregon, at Vancouver, and when the military red tape was finally gotten through with, Captain Dent, who was a brother of Mrs. U. S. Grant, the general's wife, was dispatched from Walla Walla with a command of almost eighty cavalrymen."[1]

From Fort Vancouver on 10 October, Colonel Wright informed the headquarters of the US Army that while he was at Fort Dalles on the 4th he "received intelligence of an attack upon a party of immigrants by the Mountain Snakes or Bannocks in the vicinity of the Salmon Falls."

Three men have already wandered in. The first reported all the party killed save himself. The report of the two last was received through the Commanding Officer of Fort Walla Walla on the 8th inst. in a communication to him from the Agent at the Umatilla Indian Reservation 30 miles from Fort Walla Walla. I enclose a copy. It appears from this, that eight men, one woman and four children were killed, the train & supplies etc. were taken, and the surviving members of the party dispersed. It is hoped that this report will be found to be exaggerated, though no doubt is to be entertained as to the fact that a calamity of the kind has happened. I have taken prompt measures for the relief of the survivors and have reason to expect that most, if not all, will be enabled to reach the settlements in safety.   Such relief as the Indian Agent at the Umatilla could furnish has been forwarded.   Captain Dent of the 9th Infantry, with 100 men, all mounted, will proceed rapidly along the route, and will afford such assistance to the sufferers as they may stand in need of and endeavor if season and circumstances permit, to punish the murderers.[2]

Reporting the Utter massacre to Army headquarters was undoubtedly difficult for the commander of the District of Oregon.   Colonel Wright continued his letter, attempting to explain how such a disaster could have occurred:

It will be recollected that I had reported complete success in the protection of the immigration route as one of the results of the summer's operations, and that the Snakes had been driven from the region of country lying West of the Blue Mountains and nearest the settlements.   The large body of the immigration indeed are in, safely, and owe their security unquestionably to the troops—and the exposed settlements and Indian Reservations have been preserved from serious incursions on the part of the Snakes.   Although the Commander of the Dragoon force on the road had not deemed it necessary to go as far on the route as the place probably the scene of the massacre in the discharge of his duty of escorting emigrants, this party would have experienced the benefits of his proximity and been safe, but for the convictions of the main body of the immigrants that there were no parties of immigrants in rear, and their having communicated their convictions to the Officer in Command.

The Utter wagon train was the last to cross the Snake River plains, and it had been late in the season—but not that late! Major Grier returned with his force from patrolling the trail in the Snake Country because the trains in advance of the Utter party were convinced they were the last coming to Oregon. Perhaps this was because the Utter party comprised a part of the 'larger California train' over part of their journey. In this report, Colonel Wright presented his view of the threat that the Snake Indians posed in his district (which extended from the Pacific east to the Continental Divide):

> Contrary to my reasonable anticipations that for the present there would be tranquility, although I had determined upon a campaign in the Spring, disturbances have thus occurred. Beyond the melancholy event which has taken place & occasional thefts of stock etc. no serious consequences from this renewed hostility of the Snakes, is to be apprehended to the settlements, which the means at my disposal will not avert. The Snakes (including the Root-diggers, Mountain Snakes, Bannocks etc) although composed of many bands who wander over the wide extent of country in the South East quarter of the Department are not formidable in proportion to their numbers. They have ever been a source of annoyance from their thieving propensities and their habits of lurking around immigration parties and other bands of Indians to steal animals cutting off small parties, or individuals straying from their companions. They have rarely attacked troops: but one occasion being within my recollection of so great a combination and so bold an attack of the Snakes as that upon Captain Smith's Company, during the Command in this Department of my predecessor, although acts of plunder and hostility had been committed by them during nearly the whole period of that Command. Every new success in a scheme of plunder and murder if necessary to that end of course emboldens them to a certain extent, but I do not see that any new source of danger is to arise from these Indians. Little however is known of the bands West of the Snake River in the Salmon River Country.

How little was "known of the bands" and country at that time was reflected in that last statement. Little was known of the Mountain Shoshoni north of the Snake River in the Salmon River Country. Little was known of the Northern Paiute west of the Snake River in the arid, modern-day southeastern Oregon. The Indians west of the Snake River in the Salmon River Country—the forested Wallowa Mountains—were Nez Perces, a band under the leadership of the elder Chief Joseph. The difficulty of military operations against the Snakes was outlined by Colonel Wright:

> Frequent Military expeditions must be expected among these Indians, and these involve long and painful marches through a nearly desert country. These expeditions are expensive, and harassing to the troops. Long scouts made without ever seeing at one time more than a single Indian family. The difficulty we encounter in advancing, is that we have no fixed objective point. We pursue an invisible foe, without a home, or anything tangible to strike at. The hardships these Indians undergo in war differ little from their privations in peace. Their country is nearly a desert, and they live on roots, berries, crickets & fish, and occasionally game. They unite and disperse without inconvenience. Victories can easily be gained over such an enemy, but they will rarely prove decisive. No practical result is obtained such as was gained in 1858, over the Coeur D'Alenes, Spokanes, Palouses etc. whose combination, character, & position rendered them formidable enemies. Hence their final conquest must be a work of time and patience. All that can be done now is to chastise them as well as we may, to facilitate communication by opening roads, to occupy points from which to control them, and to give protection to the annual immigration. The complete subjugation of this nomadic people will require some years: but in as much as all the Indians tribes in this country are hostile to the Snakes, the latter can look for no

friendly aid from any quarter. Hence it can never be more than a predatory warfare that these bands can wage.

The District of Utah and Colonel Wright's district had implemented a plan for conveying immigrants safely through the Snake Country. As a necessary part of the plan, the Colonel proposed the establishment of a military post in the vicinity of the old Fort Boise:

Well organized parties of immigrants who will keep together, march, camp and guard their animals as Military expeditions must necessarily do, can reach this country in safety, but this we cannot expect. If they start in large bodies, they soon break into fragments, and hence as they approach this country they readily fall a prey to any wandering bands of Indians. From the nature & vast extent of Country through which these immigrants have to pass, it will be some years before they can do so without Military escorts. Stationary Posts alone will not accomplish the end. A post has been recommended, and ordered by the Secretary of War, to be placed in the Boisee region. It will be serviceable for various reasons but will not dispense with the necessity of moving columns. Troops must travel with the immigration from the time of their leaving the Salt Lake country, until they reach the settlements. If it were announced that Military escorts would leave Utah about the 15th of July & 15th of August annually to meet escorts from Fort Walla Walla, or the new Post when established, about the 15th of August and the 15th of September, it is believed that all who desired it could easily avail themselves of such opportunities to travel in safety, and thus the yearly immigration be perfectly protected. Small parties of the Snakes, in numbers sometimes not exceeding from 2 to 5 have been lurking around and have stolen stock from the Warm Spring Reservation, where are Wasco & other Indians their enemies, and where are the Snake captives taken during the summer. The Wascoes are amply able to protect themselves from these Marauders, but are afraid of them, and difficulty was apprehended by the Supt. in getting the Indians on to the Reservation. I therefore upon the requisition of Mr. Geary, Supt. sent a detachment to the Warm Spring Reservation of 18 men under Lieutenant Gregg, 1st Dragoons, who will winter there and reassure the friendly Indians and protect the Reserve.

I suggest as the country in the Boisee region is almost entirely without resources that $150,000 at least be included in the estimate of the Quartermaster Department for building a Post of five Companies there. The transportation of rations, supplies etc. must likewise be increased should a Post be established. Estimates in forms will be submitted in due course.

In reporting the news of the Utter massacre to Headquarters, US Army (in the foregoing, lengthy letter), the old soldier had taken the opportunity to explain how the disaster could occur—but, of course, offered no excuse. The makeup of the army relief force and the Army's plans were explained by Colonel Wright in an 18 October letter to the governor of Oregon:

Your communication of the 8th inst to the Senate of Oregon has come to my notice through the public prints. I have presumed that it would afford you satisfaction to be advised of the steps I have taken with regard to the rescue of the remnant of the immigrant party who escaped from the recent massacre in the vicinity of the Salmon Falls, and what operations are in contemplation for next spring and summer to remedy the state of things which formed the topic of your message.

You are already informed that the reports at first received with regard to this massacre were exaggerated. They came through parties eager to escape at the first show of danger, who had they remained and assisted their comrades might with them have saved their train and some of the lives. The last report was through the commanding officer of Fort Walla Walla, from Mr. B. M. Dawes resident at the Umatilla Reservation. I enclose a slip from the Statesman of October 15 which is substantially the same as that report. This reduces materially the number of the killed and leaves room for hope that most of the dispersed may yet reach the settlements. Parties which Mr. Dawes says he dispatched to the assistance of the survivors have returned, I am informed without falling in with any. It is not to be presumed, however, that these parties pursued the search to any great distance. I received information, on the 16th inst. that five more of the surviving immigrants have come into Fort Walla Walla.[3]

This report of the arrival of five more survivors proved to be erroneous. Colonel Wright continued by informing the governor of Oregon that "acting upon the first intelligence I issued the following directives:"

A detachment of Troops from Fort Walla Walla will proceed immediately under Captain Frederick T. Dent 9th Infy to the scene of the reported massacre of Emigrants in the vicinity of the Salmon Falls of the Snake River to obtain any survivors there may prove to be in the hands of the Indians, and if season and opportunity permit to punish the aggressors. The detachment will be composed of Company E. 1st dragoons and a detail from Company I 1st dragoons sufficient to make a total of sixty dragoons, and one subaltern and forty enlisted men to be selected for service from Companies B and E 9th Infantry. The infantry will be mounted on mules. Forty days' rations and an ample supply of ammunition will be taken with the command.

Included in this letter to the governor was an excerpt of Wright's above report to Army headquarters, on his plans for protecting future emigrants. The Colonel concluded by observing that

> steps for the establishment of a post at Boise were deferred by the late commander of this department until the result of certain explanations was ascertained, with the approval of the Secretary of War. No appropriation for building a post there, however, passed last winter.
>
> Troops will be sent into the field against the Snakes early in the spring and will be prepared to carry on the War vigorously.
>
> In conclusion, I have to assure you that the military resources at my disposal will be promptly and actively employed whenever the protection of citizens from the hostilities of Indians or the punishment of Indians for past outrages as a preventive against future hostility may render it necessary. Unless disturbances occur in another quarter, not now to be anticipated, which may cause a division of the military forces under my command, I have troops enough to secure the immigrant route within the limits of the department from danger on the part of the Snake Indians. All that is necessary is the money to furnish the transportation of supplies indispensable, and for the establishment at Fort Boise.

The people in the East were later informed of the Army relief force plans, via the *New York Times*. The *Times* also reported that "Major ENOCK STEEN, First Dragoons, is assigned to the command of Fort Walla Walla" and that the "Warm Spring Reservation is to be protected by Lieut. GREGG and eighteen privates of Company H, First Dragoons."[4] The *Pioneer and Democrat* of Olympia, W.T. also reported on this: "Army Intelligence.—By command of Col. Wright, Lieut. Gregg, with twenty dragoons, has taken up quarters at the Warm Springs Reservation, there to be ready to repel a possible attack from bands of Snake Indians."[5] The information was correct as Second Lieutenant David Mc. M. Gregg and twenty-six enlisted men left Fort Dalles 11 October on detached service at Warm Springs Indian Reservation. This was two days after Lieutenant Lyons from Vancouver Barracks passed through Fort Dalles with a 3rd Infantry escort for the Fort Benton Wagon Road.

Major Enoch Steen, 1st Dragoons, was the commander of Fort Dalles. Earlier, in May, he had been detached to form the expedition to open a wagon road from Lake Harney to Eugene City and returned in September. Now, 4 October 1860, Major Steen was officially transferred to Fort Walla Walla to assume command.[6] He had already been working closely with the dragoons there.

] The Relief Force [

There were thirteen officers of the garrison at Fort Walla Walla in the summer of 1860; five had their families there. Colonel George Wright (West Point, 1822) was Commander of the 9th Infantry Regiment (transferred from Fort Dalles in June, 1859). The 1860 Federal Census listed Wright as being born in Vermont fifty-five years before. His wife, Margaret W., was with him at Walla Walla (they moved to Fort Vancouver in July when Wright assumed command of the Department of Oregon).

Also at Walla Walla was Thomas F. Wright, twenty-nine, a clerk or agent of the Quartermaster Department. Major William Grier (West Point, 1835) of the 1st Dragoons, age forty-seven and born in Pennsylvania, was with his wife in this remote frontier Northwest. Captain Frederick Tracy Dent of the 9th Infantry was thirty-seven in 1860. He had his wife and two children there. He was born in Missouri; graduated from the Military Academy in 1843 (his classmate, Hiram Ulysses Simpson Grant, married his sister, Julia Dent).

The wife and child of Second Lieutenant Robert H. Anderson were also there. Anderson, of the 9th Infantry, was born in Georgia twenty-four years before. Among the other junior officers was twenty-five-year-old Second Lieutenant Marcus A. Reno who was born in Illinois. He and Robert Anderson had served in the Army three years now following their graduation from West Point.[7]

It would be three weeks after Colonel Wright wrote the letter to Oregon's governor that Captain Frederick T. Dent made his report, the day following the return of the Army relief expedition to Fort Walla Walla:

FORT WALLA WALLA, <u>November 8, 1860</u>.
CAPTAIN: I have the honor to report for the information of the colonel commanding the department of Oregon, that on the evening of October 4, 1860, being at Fort Dalles, Oregon, I received from yourself department orders No. 105, directing me to take command of an expedition to be fitted out at Fort Walla-Walla for the purpose of recovering or rescuing any survivors that might be of the massacre of emigrants which took place on the 9th and 10th of September, 1860, in the vicinity of Salmon Falls on Snake river.

I left Fort Dalles at 12 a.m. on the 5th, and reached this place on the 9th of October, and presented orders No. 105 to Capt. A. J. Smith, 1st dragoons, then in command, who immediately ordered the organization of my command, in accordance with those orders, and so prompt was the action of all departments that I was enabled to move my party out from the post to a camp on the Tumalum on the evening of the 11th of October.

The command as organized consisted of—

	Officers.	Enlisted men.
Company E, 1st dragoons....	1	40
Detachment of company J, 1st dragoons.	0	20
Company B, 9th infantry..........	1	20
Detachment of Company E, 9th infantry..	1	20
Field and staff......................	1	0
	4	100

Mr. T. Wright, agent of quartermaster's department, in charge of train and public property.

Captain F. T. Dent commanding.

Assistant Surgeon L. Taylor, medical officer.

Second Lieutenant M. A. Reno, commanding dragoons.

Second Lieutenant R. H. Anderson, commanding infantry.

The infantry were mounted on mules, and our stores, ammunition, and camp equipage transported on pack mules.[D]

The relief expedition traveled due south from Fort Walla Walla to strike the Oregon Trail. Agent Abbott visited the expedition when it passed through the Umatilla Indian Reservation:

Captain Dent, 9th Infty, commanding a detachment of troops, left his camp at the foot of the Blue mountains, about five miles from this agency, on the 14th of the month, en route to the scene of the massacre. He is a prompt, energetic, and efficient officer, and is actuated by a proper spirit, as are also the officers and men under him; and if it is in the power of man to accomplish aught for the benefit of any of the survivors of the party, if any exist, he will do it. I sent Jacob Keith, who is now in my employ, with the expedition.[8]

Abbott, in writing the above on 30 October, had the Reith's name wrong but identified Jacob correctly. In Abbott's later account (published in 1908) he recorded that Joseph Reith "was the older and stronger" brother and that Joe Reith was the brother that went with the Army relief force; this was incorrect. In this later account Abbot also wrote that the expedition "crossed the Blue Mountains, passed through Grand Ronde valley, the Powder River and Burnt River valleys under the guidance of an old Scotch mountaineer named Craig, who

lived among the Nez Perce Indians at Lapwai."⁹   William
Craig, a former fur trapper, was fifty-three in 1860 and was
born in Greenbrier County, Virginia.   He and his Nez Perce
wife, Isabel, had settled on Lapwai Creek, shortly after the
Reverend Henry Spalding established his mission at Lapwai in
1836. By 1846 the Craigs had established an Appaloosa horse
ranch there.* Craig sometimes wintered in Walla Walla, where
he was postmaster in 1858-59.¹⁰

The progress of the Army relief force did not please Captain Dent.

Our march was slow, and the command moved together until we reached Powder river, on the 17th of October. Not being satisfied with the speed we were
making, I determined to scout the country forward
with strong parties unencumbered, and accordingly
ordered Lieutenant Reno, with forty men, 1st dragoons, and two guides, with ten mules lightly packed,
to scout thoroughly the Burnt river and its vicinity, the
main command following him as fast as it could.ᴰ

---

*William Craig is considered to be Idaho's first permanent white settler. Craig's Mountain is named for him.

EIGHT

Army Rescue

Old Mr. Munson and Chaffee, with the Reith brothers, had attempted to continue on the Oregon Trail for help. They had given out though, a short distance up Burnt River, and the Reith boys had continued on. Captain Dent's troops found the two who stayed, in a very emaciated condition, still on Burnt River. "On the evening of the 19th Lieutenant Reno discovered on a small branch of Burnt river* two emigrants almost naked, without fire, and starving; the names of these two, as given me by themselves are Civilian G. Munson and Charles M. Chaffee. Lieutenant Reno clothed them and supplied them with food, and leaving a corporal and ten men with them, he proceeded rapidly to the front."ᴰ An expressman from the relief force said the two presented the most heartrending sight he had ever seen: men, living skeletons, weeping for joy at their deliverance from hunger.[1]

The remainder of Lieutenant Reno's dragoon force searched the Trail to the east. Later that night they arrived where the town of Huntington now stands.

> On arriving at the place on Burnt river where the road leaves it, and having found no trace of the remainder of the emigrants, Lieutenant Reno put in camp twenty-five of his party, and with five men and Mr. Craigie, [William Craig] the guide, proceeded riding day and night to the Malheur; having made no discoveries on the Malheur, Lieutenant Reno returned toward Burnt river.ᴰ

*In the vicinity of Dixie Creek, Exit 338 of Interstate 84.

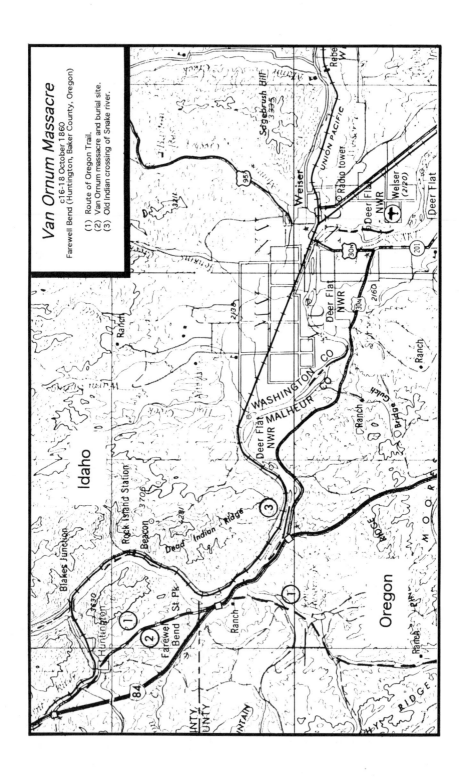

Van Ornum Massacre

c16-18 October 1860
Farewell Bend (Huntington, Baker County, Oregon)

(1) Route of Oregon Trail.
(2) Van Ornum massacre and burial site.
(3) Old Indian crossing of Snake river.

Those in the relief efforts, of the Umatilla Agency and now the Army, were unaware that the emigrant families had stopped on the Owyhee. It was assumed that they would be much further along the Trail. The Van Ornum party had stayed with the other emigrants at the camp on the Owyhee River for two and a half weeks. They had then left that camp, after the Shoshone Indians discovered them and became threatening. In the next few days the Van Ornum party had traveled on to the Burnt River.

Captain Dent described Lieutenant Reno's search for the emigrant families as he returned on the Trail toward Farewell Bend:

> At some points on the road finding tracks of women and children, their trail passing over rocky ground, and rain having fallen on it since made, it was hard to know until he came to where the emigrant road between Malheur and Burnt river touches on Snake river; here the trail was fresh and his hopes were roused of speedily finding them; the daylight was nearly gone, but the search continued, and when he proceeded to within two miles of the camp he had left on Burnt river, he came on, at a short distance from the road, and in the sage brush a scene of murder and mutilation, only to be found where the warwhoop has signalled the scalping-knife's deadly work; gleaming in the moonlight, dead, stripped, and mutilated, lay the bodies of six persons.

The members of the Van Ornum party were found on the high ground between the two rivers, two miles northwest of Farewell Bend. The remains found were identified by the Reith brother accompanying the expedition as those of Alexis Van Ornum and his wife Abigail, both thirty-nine years of age; their sixteen year old son, Mark; Samuel Gleason; and Charles and Henry Utter. The bodies were brutally beaten and scored with knives. The arms of Mrs. Van Ornum were tied; she had been whipped, scalped, and otherwise abused by her

Van Ornum Massacre

Burial site of Van Ornum Party marked by a small iron cross. (By permission from Chris Moore, Ontario, Oregon.)

Huntington Hill

Looking toward Van Ornum Massacre site on south side of US 30 toward top of hill between Farewell Bend and Huntington, Oregon.

murderers.[2] The "boys, Charles and Henry Otter, had been killed by arrows. Mr. Vanorman, Marcus Vanorman, and Gleason had their throats cut, and besides were pierced by numerous arrows. They appeared to have been dead from four to six days; the wolves had not yet molested them; decomposition was going on however, and Lieutenant Reno buried them."[D]

The bodies were buried where they were found.[*] Mrs. Van Ornum's body was laid to rest four and a half feet deep, separate from the common grave containing the five remains of the men and boys.[3] Emeline wrote (in 1891 in Wisconsin):

> Their bodies lay unburied, showing marks of torture, too develish for any human beings to inflict except Indians.
>
> Let those who have never suffered as I have pity the fate of the noble red man of the forest. My pity all goes out for their poor unfortunate victims, and I can never look even upon one of our poor degraded harmless Winnebagoes without such feelings as I do not like to entertain towards any of God's created beings, and I almost doubt if they are a part of our great Maker's work. . . .
>
> The dragoons commenced to bury the dead, who it was very evident had been dead but a short time, but the Reath boy begged of them not to stop there for the night, as it was getting late in the afternoon, but to push on for he told them there were certainly more somewhere and it was possible they might find them alive.

Captain Dent arrived immediately afterward at Lieutenant Reno's camp, and found him:

---

*According to Frank L. Tyler of Nampa (whose mother was a niece of John, Joseph, and Michael Myers), the site is near the top of the southeast side of the hill, along old U.S. 30, between Farewell Bend and Huntington. In an article by Chris Moore in the *Ontario Argus-Observer*, 13 March 1969, the Van Ornum party "were overtaken by Indians near present U. S. Highway 30 about one fourth mile west of the [highway near the] summit of the Huntington Hill. . . . A small iron cross in a semi-circular cove in the side of a hill to the south of the highway marks the spot." The simple cross was placed there by P. D. Wood of Huntington who located the graves and the massacre site.

Snake River

Looking upstream from Farewell Bend toward old Indian crossing of Snake River. Interstate 84 in the foreground.

Old Indian Crossing of Snake River

Looking north at Indian Head Mountain. Taken Thanksgiving Day 1992 after years of drought reduced Brownlee Reservoir to reveal the crossing.

absent on a scout with a guide and ten men, he having
found in the vicinity of the place where the Vanormans
were killed a trail of Indians with whom he supposed
might be some of the Vanorman family; this he supposed from finding a small barefoot track among the
moccasin tracks. He followed the trail to where it
went into the Salmon River mountains, first crossing
the Snake river at their bases;* having no means of
crossing Snake river which is here very rapid and
deep, he returned to camp and reported to me. I
deemed it best not to pursue the trail at that time, as I
had learned from Mr. Munson during that day that on
Snake river, some fifteen miles beyond Owyhee, he
had parted with the Vanorman, Chase, Myers, and
some of the Trimble and Otter families. A long time
had elapsed since he left them, yet I had hopes of
finding some of them alive, as the Vanormans who
had evidently parted from the others had been so recently killed; I therefore determined to push forward
with all haste. Lieutenant Anderson, 9th infantry,
with thirty-five men and light packs, moved forward
with orders to make a thorough search of the Malheur
and Owyhee, the main command moving on the same
route.[D]

]   Rescue On The Owyhee   [

"Someone was coming. All got to their feet, fearing Indians, but by this time they had seen" Emeline Trimble "and
were riding fast, and all saw they were soldiers."[MM] The
mounted infantry had traveled all night without resting. To
Emeline there was:

no doubt but we owed our lives to that night's work of
those brave tender-hearted men for we were sure that

---

*This would be the 'ages-old Indian crossing' of the Snake River, upstream from Farewell Bend at the
south end of Indian Head Mountain (Dead Indian Ridge), which lies to the west of the Weiser Flat.

the Indians were on their way to kill us when scared away by the approaching soldiers.

About ten o'clock in the morning we saw signal fires off a few miles from our camp and we knew that either they were coming to kill us or help was close at hand and strange as it may seem to my readers my heart was so benumbed by my terrible sufferings that I hardly cared which it was. I was alone in the world and had suffered enough in the past months to change me from a light-hearted child into a broken-hearted woman, and my wish was that I might lie down and die, and join my kindred in a world free from cares and troubles like those I had passed through. I was out after fuel as usual, when I saw the soldiers coming but was too weak to feel much joy at seeing them. They rode up to me and a few dismounted, and coming to me asked if I did not want something to eat. I answered that I did not care. I shall never forget the pitying looks bent on me by those strong men. Tears stood in every eye as one of the officers gave me a part of a biscuit. I ate that, but did not care for more, but in a few days I was hungry enough to eat anything. I could not have lived many days longer if help had not reached us.

The *Oregon Argus* reported that when the soldiers came into the little valley where the camp was, the first one they saw was "Miss Trimble, who had wandered off a few hundred yards, gathering something. (She is the young lady who picked up an infant at the time of the massacre, and carried it along till it died; she also defended the wagon some time with an ax in hand)." Lieutenant Anderson spoke to her and asked if she was hungry. "No sir, not much." "Are you not afraid of the Indians?" he asked. "No sir," she replied. She seemed to be half out of her mind, but took everything quite calmly.[M]

The pitiful, starved emigrants saw that the fast-riding party of soldiers coming up was not very large, but strong enough not to fear the Indians. Mrs. Myers cried to the others, "They

have come. They have come." They tried to run out to the soldiers, but were so weak they fell to the ground. They were
weeping, and trying to shout, but could not make much
noise.ᴹᴹ ᴵᴹ

When Lieutenant Anderson went into that little willow
camp, the children hung on to him begging for food. "Bread,
bread," they cried. What a horrid sight was presented to the
soldiers when they viewed that Owyhee camp. The emigrants
cried out that they were starving, and begged for something to
eat. The soldiers threw themselves down and wept, and it
was as much as Lieutenant Anderson could do to keep them
from giving food to the starving survivors.ᴹ

One private, jumped from his horse and grabbed his
saddle bags, containing his rations, among other
things bread and crackers, and dumped it on the
ground. He was cursed for a fool by the captain
[Lieutenant Anderson] and ordered to pick it all up,
but was not quite quick enough to get it all, as some of
them already had it in their hands, but it was all taken
from us by the captain, and how disappointed I
[Margaret] was, not understanding it was kindness
and that it would have killed us to have eaten what we
wanted. This was about two hours before sunset I
think.ᴹᴹ

Lieutenant Anderson made the soldiers shut their saddlebags, declaring, "It will kill them if we let them overeat."ᴵᴹ
"What is this?" he inquired as he scrutinized what was cooking
on the fire. He received no reply to his query. He carried it to
the bank of the Owyhee and threw it into the stream.⁴

The Lieutenant allowed the soldiers to give the survivors a
few mouthfuls of food. In a short time they were able to move
around. Then they were picked up and placed on the soldiers'
mounts. They rode off a little way and made camp. Coffee
was made and some soup. Every two hours the survivors
were fed a little. It was a happy but nearly disastrous night for

the starving people as their bodies tried to adjust to the food.[5] Margaret's

> baby sister nearly died. They only gave her a teaspoonful of weak arrowroot gruel, a few times through the night, but the poor little stomach could not retain that, and those hardy soldiers worked all night to keep her alive. I hope God rewarded them. Carolyn was that baby, and for two years she was little and pale and thin. My brother also was very near gone. His eyes were glazed, and all desire for food was gone. The soldiers said he would not have lived through the night, but the warmth of the blankets and a little gruel kept him alive. They thought none of us would have lived more than three days.

From the first Indian attack on the emigrant train, until the arrival of the relieving party at the willow camp on the Owyhee, was forty-five days.

> On the morning of the 25th of October, when en route to the Owyhee from the Malheur, I [Captain Dent] received an express from Lieutenant Anderson, informing me that the evening before he had found on the Owyhee twelve emigrants alive and five dead; those still alive were keeping life in them by eating those who had died. I will not attempt to describe the scene of horror this camp presented, even when I reached it at 12 o'clock that day; those who were still alive were skeletons with life in them; their frantic cries for food rang in our ears incessantly; food was given them every hour in small quantities, but for days the cry was still kept up by the children.
>
> Those found and relieved by Lieutenant Anderson, were: Mr. Joseph Myers, Mary E. Myers his wife, and their five children, Isabella, Margaret, Eugene, Harriet, and Carry Myers; Mrs. Elizabeth

Chase, and daughter, Mary Chase; and Miss Emeline Trimble.

The dead in the camp (consumed) were: Mr. Daniel Chase, and his two sons, Daniel and Albert Chase; Elizabeth Trimble; and an infant of Mrs. Otter, half sister of Miss Trimble.[D]

Those rescued were not entirely without clothes (as had been represented), but were scantily dressed. The survivors were nothing but skin and bone, and the children, so weak they would tumble down when they tried to run. Their fingers were like birds' claws, eyes hollow-looking, cheeks sunken; they seemed to be half out of their senses; they would sit there and quarrel about who had the biggest piece of meat, and fuss about any little foolish thing. Sometimes they would be in fine spirits, talk about good old times, assistance coming, of their plans and prospects when they got into the settlements; then they would realize their true situation, and commence crying.[M]

The survivors told the soldiers about the several visits from the Indians and how the Indians later disappeared from their camp across the Snake River. The soldiers surmised that the Indians had followed the Van Ornum party and killed them for some mysterious reason of their own.[MM] (The Indians' last visit to the families was three days after the Van Ornum party had left; if the Indians had not known of the departure of Van Ornums before, they did then; that was when they had become agitated about soldiers coming.)

The soldiers were shown the track where Joseph Myers had found Christopher Trimble's locks of hair. In following up this sign and searching over the area, they discovered Christopher's body. They found a head, an arm, and some things showing the boy had been killed, but the soldiers told the survivors that they figured that when the Indians abandoned their camp, they might have started Christopher back to the families' camp on the Owyhee and that the coyotes got him. The survivors had heard the coyotes a few times, but had not seen any. If they had, they would have tried to kill one to eat.[M MM]

An hour or two before my [Captain Dent's] arrival at Lieutenant Anderson's camp, he found the remains of Christopher Trimble, who had been murdered by the Indians; his body had been much disturbed by the wolves, but sufficient remained to identify it. These remains were found a short distance beyond the Owyhee. This boy, of eleven years of age, deserves especial mention. He had killed several Indians in the fight; he left the fugitives and went forward to the Malheur, where he obtained of Chaffee some horse flesh, which he took back to the women and children; he then became a prisoner voluntarily with the Indians, in order that he might get salmon taken to the camp, and did succeed in so doing and in going with the Indians there. Two weeks had elapsed since his last visit; it must have been at that time that he was killed.

Lieutenant Anderson's party buried the remains found in this camp, and also the remains of young Trimble.

]   The Expedition's Return   [

When the main force, under Captain Dent, arrived, the survivors were moved away from their camp on the Owyhee. The entire force prepared the survivors for the trip to Fort Walla Walla. An Indian runner was dispatched to the Fort to have ambulances and supplies sent out to meet the expedition. On 26 October the soldiers and survivors remained in camp. They constructed litters and panniers for transporting the women and children.[DE]

The soldiers commenced at once making preparations for the return to the fort. They took us about three miles from our camp the next day after their arrival and went into camp there and waited for us to get ready. They told us to make some skirts out of blankets which they gave us, and we wore some of their underclothes, and their short blue coats, which were comfortable, for it was getting to be cold days and nights, as it was now the 25th or 26th of October. I [Emeline] cannot speak half well enough of the soldiers to express their kind and gentlemanly treatment of us, and I shall carry through life the recollection not only of the kindness but even of the features of those large-hearted soldiers, and I almost think I should recognize any of them should I ever see them.

In conversation with Joseph Myers, Captain Dent learned that when the Van Ornums left the Owyhee the party consisted of ten persons. The relief force had found all of the party excepting four Van Ornum children, three girls and one boy. The eldest girl, thirteen year old Eliza, was thought to be fourteen or fifteen years old; the next one, Minerva, twelve or thirteen. Reuben was eight years old and the youngest Van Ornum, Lucinda, was probably six. Captain Dent now felt assured that their conjecture was correct, that the Van Ornum children were captives with the Indians, and Lieutenant Reno and the scout, William Craig, had followed their trail to where they crossed Snake river at Indian Head Mountain. Captain Dent was determined to follow that trail on the Army's return to the vicinity of Burnt River, and recover the children or learn their fate.[6] Dent had also learned:

that all who had left the wagons were with us on, or had passed, the Owyhee, and that all who remained at the train were dead before the fugitives left. To save the lives of those we had recovered now became our paramount duty. Officers and men gave them the larger portion of the clothing and blankets they had brought for their own use, yet I feared we should lose some of them from the cold. The snow was all around us on the hills. I therefore determined to return to Burnt river, and on Saturday, the 27th, in a heavy storm of rain and sleet, we commenced our march. Four of the children were in narrow hampers on pack

9 September 1860 (Su, Day 1)

Lewis Lawson		Killed
Pvt William Utley		Killed
Pvt Charles Kishnell	German	Killed

10 September (M, Day 2)

Judson Cressey		Killed
John W. Myers		Killed
Mary Utter	about 23	Killed
Elijah Utter		Killed
Wesley Utter	5	Killed
Emma Utter		Killed
Abagel Trimble Utter	33	Killed
Abby Utter		Killed

c23 September (Su, Day 15)

Sgt Charles Schamberg	27	Killed
Pvt Theodore Murdock	24	Killed

30 September (Su Day 22)

Pvt. Henry Snyder	29	Saved

2 October (Tu, Day 24)

Jacob Rieth	22	Saved
Joseph Rieth		Saved

c4 October (Th, Day 26)

Daniel Chase		Died

c7 October (Su, Day 29)

Christopher Trimble	10	Killed

c13 October (Sa, Day 35)

Elizabeth Trimble	9	Died of starvation

c16-18 October (Day 38-40)

Alexus Van Ornum	39	Killed
Marcus Van Ornum	17	Killed
Samuel Gleason	young man	Killed
Charles Utter	a lad	Killed
Henry Utter	about 12	Killed
Abagail Van Ornum		Killed

Fate of the Utter Party.   (Complied by Author).

c18 October (Th, Day 40)
  Susan Utter   1   Died of starvation
c19 October (F, Day 41)
  Daniel Chase, Jr.   8   Died of starvation
19 October (F, Day 41)

c18 October (Th, Day 40)		
Susan Utter	1	Died of starvation
c19 October (F, Day 41)		
Daniel Chase, Jr.	8	Died of starvation
19 October (F, Day 41)		
Goodsel Munson	old gentleman	Rescued
Charles M. Chaffee	18	Rescued
c21 October (Su, Day 43)		
Albert Chase	6	Died of starvation
24 October (W, Day 46)		
Joseph Myer		Rescued
Mary Myers	28	Rescued
Isabella Myers	10	Rescued
Margaret Myers	7	Rescued
Eugene Myers	5	Rescued
Harriet Myers (lame)	3	Rescued
Carrie Myer	not yet 1	Rescued
Elizabeth Chase		Rescued
Mary Chase	2	Rescued
Emeline Trimble	14	Rescued
Missing (Captured by Indians):		
Lucinda Van Ornum	6	
Eliza Van Ornum	13	
Minerva Van Ornum	probably 12	
Reuben Van Ornum	8	

Killed	20
Died	6
Missing	4
Saved	3
Rescued	<u>12</u>
	44

Fate of the Utter Party (Cont.).   (Complied by Author).

mules, and two with their mothers in a mule litter. One of the women was carried on a hand litter; this I abandoned, and had her placed on a mule with a man on each side to hold her. It was a weary and painful march to them.

Those survivors who had strength enough were put on mules. The women were too weak to ride. They were carried on litters made of blankets, swung between two mules arranged in tandem. The soldiers made saddlebags, or a two-pouch arrangement, that hung across their saddles and put a child in each one—one to a side. It was uncomfortable riding for the children. Mrs. Chase and Emeline changed off, at first, and each rode a part of the time on the litter. It was very hard for Mrs. Chase to travel other than on a litter. She was thrown off from the mule she was riding and hurt. Emeline then gave up her place on the litter to Mrs. Chase.[7]

On the 27th we arrived on Burnt river, and to my regret, I [Captain Dent] was forced to abandon all idea of a pursuit of the murderers of the Vanorman family, as the snow had fallen heavily in the mountains and obliterated their trail. This being the case, and the snow still falling on us and around us, I determined to push homeward and cross the Blue mountains before the snow became too deep for marching over those mountains.

The next day Captain Dent wrote a preliminary report of the rescue to the District of Oregon Headquarters:

> Homeward bound
> Camp on Burnt River
> Oct 28th 1860.

Capt.
    I know that the Colonel commanding is anxious to hear to what extent we have succeeded.

Our success has been greater than I expected. I shall, as soon as I reach Fort Walla Walla make an official report and give details. Here I will only mention that I have in my camp twelve of the emigrants that we have rescued from horrors that will not admit of relation. Suffice it to say that when found on the Owyhee they were living on the putrified corpses of those who had died and when found by us had consumed five human bodies (children and husband) The living that are with us are.

> Mr Chaffee
> Mr Munson
> Mr Myers
> Mrs Myers
> 5 children of Mr & Mrs Myers
> Mrs Chase and one child
> Miss Emaline Trimble

Two brothers by the name of Reitt came on to the Umatilla Agency.

We found murdered by the indians near the Camp.

> Mr Vanornan
> Mrs Vanornan
> Mr Gleason
> Mr Charles Otter
> Mr Henry Otter
> Mr Marcus Vanornan (aged 17)

These were found and buried by Lieutenant Reno who also found and rescued messrs Chaffee and Munson. Lieutenant Anderson found and relieved Mr Myers and family, Mrs Chase and child, and Miss Trimble: he also found the remains of Henry [*sic*] Trimble. All of Vanornan's family were not killed I am inclined to think that four of his children are in the hands of the indians who have fled into the mountains on the other side of Snake river. We can now account for all.

Killed with the Wagons.	Killed by the Indians on the road	Died in Camp and eaten
Lewis Lawson	Alexis Vanornan	Mr Chase
William Otley	Abigal Vanornan	Danl Chase } chil-
Charles Kishnell	Marcus Vanornan	Albert Chase } dren
Judson Cressy	Charles Otter	Elizabeth Trimble
John W Myers	Henry Otter	(5)Infant of Mrs Otters
Mr Otter	Christopher Trimble	Supposed prisoners in
Mrs Otter	Samuel Gleason	the hands of the Inds
Mary Otter	(7)_____	Eliza, Minerva,
Emma Otter		Lucinda, &
Wesley Otter		(4)Rueben Vanornen
Abbey Otter		Shamberg & Murdock
(11)_____		(2) Comrades of
		Schnieder Lost
		in mtns of Malheur.

15   Saved
11   Killed with train
7   Killed by Indians and buried by us
5   Died in camp and eaten
4   Supposed to be prisoners
2   Lost in the mountains
44   the original number in train.

The snows are all around us and our emigrants are much reduced but I hope to get in by the 7th of November.

In great haste and very cold
Fred T. Dent
Capt 9th Infy
Comdg Expedition[8]

On the 31st the expedition spent the night at Spring Branch; they continued on the next day. After traveling a few days the government ambulances sent by Major Steen from Fort Walla Walla met the relief force at the Grand Ronde River. The wagons had an abundance of clothing, blankets, and provisions, sent to the emigrants by the officers, women, laundresses, and men of the post. The survivors now had clothes to keep them warm and an easy wagon to ride in.[9]

NINE

News Of The Rescue

As the Army relief expedition was slowly returning with the survivors of the Utter massacre, another agency of the government, the Bureau of Indian Affairs, was keeping abreast of the events. A month had elapsed since Snyder and the Reith brothers reached civilization. At the end of October George Abbott was writing Edward R. Geary, his superior in Portland:

Umatilla Agency Ogn
October 30th 1860

Sir

Your communication dated Octr 10th authorizing and directing me to act on behalf of the Indian Department in the case of the late massacre of immigrants by the Snake Indians was received duly, and I have to inform you that your instructions were anticipated to the best that could be done by this agency in affording relief to any who might have survived; but in vain as our relief party found none of the immigrants.

The following are the particulars of that horrid affair as far as heard from, up to the present. . . .

. . . I sent Jacob Keith, [Reith] who is now in my employ, with the expedition. I have this day sent an express to Walla-Walla to ascertain if any intelligence has been received at that point from Captain Dent, and will give you the result in this communication.

This is a most sad affair, but I will refrain from comment, and confine my report to facts as they are developed. The foregoing particulars of the massacre

I get from the Keith brothers, and the fate of the two discharged soldiers is given by Snyder. . . .
P.S. Nov 1, 1860

The express has just arrived from Walla Walla with intelligence of the recovery by Capt Dent of twelve of the lost immigrants. I refer you to the enclosed letter of Capt Smith.

[Enclosed]

Ft. Walla Walla W.T.
Oct. 31, 1860

Dear Sir

An express has just arrived from Capt Dent bringing in the gratifying news of the recovery of twelve of the lost emigrants—4 men 2 women and 6 children. They were found in a deplorable condition quite naked and starving, having subsisted on berries and as a last on the remains of some of their own party—who had died some days previous. Capt Dent will be on the Umatilla about Sunday or Monday next [7th or 8th] where you can get the full particulars from him. We send out three wagons tomorrow with vegetables clothing and other articles for the sufferers and hope to give them a warm reception.

There is no truth in the reports that two women came in on dry creek.

Yours truly,
A. J. Smith
Capt

G. H. Abbott Esq
Umatilla Agency
Oregon[1]

The news brought to Fort Walla Walla of the relief expedition's success spread quickly. A Mr. O. C. Harcum sent the following letter which appeared in the *Portland Advertiser* on 6 November 1860. It also appeared in the *Oregon City Argus* on 10 November; the Olympia, W.T. *Pioneer and Democrat* on

16 November; and on the 29th, a garbled version was in the *New York Times*.

WALLA WALLA, Nov. 1, 1860

ED. ADVERTISER;—Sad but yet gratifying news I have to communicate to you. An express from Captain Dent arrived at this place yesterday, with letters from officers in the expedition. I have been permitted to make the following extracts:

"Burnt River, Oct. 28th. We are here with the snow all around us upon the hills, but I have no fears of being hemmed in by it. I am on my march back to Walla-Walla. We have been successful. We have with us twelve of the immigrants, viz: Mr. Jeffrey, Mr. Munson, Mr. Myers and wife, and five children, Mrs. Chase and child, and Miss Trimble."

Another letter states:

"We are homeward bound after a successful tramp. We have been as far as the Owyhee, and rescued twelve of the emigrants alive, buried eight, and can now account for all that were in the train."

Mr. [Michael] Myers, brother of the rescued Myers, started to meet his brother and family this morning. A supply train and ambulance were immediately sent out from the Fort with blankets, clothing, fresh vegetables, beef, and other necessaries, which will meet them near the Grand Ronde about the 3rd or 4th inst.

By the 7th or 8th, we expect the train will arrive at the Fort.

The official report, giving details, will be made out in a few days.

The details are of the most heart-rending character. They were in a perfect state of nudity—having been stripped by the Indians and left to perish. For ten days previous to their discovery they had subsisted upon *human flesh*, the bodies of those who had perished. Mrs. Chase had fed upon the dead body of her husband. A private letter says that on the evening of the 27th Oct. [24th] an officer with a detachment in advance of the main party, found near a small stream the women and children naked, in a state of starvation, and greatly emaciated, so much so that their bones almost protruded through the skin. The women and children, on seeing their rescuers, fell upon their knees, and by the most piteous wailing, implored food. The stout hearts of the soldiers were softened to the most touching emotions of pity, which was immediately followed by dire revenge towards the red skins.

On receiving the intelligence at the Fort the sensation felt was such as humanity alone can experience, the conduct of Maj. Stein, the officer in command, was prompt, and every comfort of the fort which could be transported, was quickly dispatched to the scene of the suffering. The wives of the officers purchased every description of clothing requisite for the women and children of the train. A physician, with medicines, &c, accompanied the supply train.

More full accounts will be given when the train arrives. Meantime, I trust the people of the Valley will suspend their judgment upon the cause both remote and intermediate of this dire calamity.[2]

A correspondent of the *Oregon City Argus*, Len, intercepted Harcum's letter at the steamboat landing on the Upper Columbia and added some additional and inaccurate information of his own:

WALLULA, Nov. 2, 1860.
ED. ARGUS: The survivors of the immigrant party lately massacred by the Snake Indians were found on the 28th Oct. by Capt. Dent, who had gone in search of them. An express from him arrived here on the 31st. No particulars are given—though the whole party are accounted for.

The survivors, 12 in number, were found on Burnt River, destitute of everything, except life—8 had died of starvation, and the living were subsisting on the bodies of the dead. It seems after the Indians ceased the massacre, they plundered the party of everything, stripping even the clothing from the women and children, and left them to perish and starve in the wilderness without food or clothes. Those who had straggled in might well report, that they were the only survivors. They are expected here on the 8th. The expressman says they presented the most heart-rending sight he ever saw—men, living skeletons, weeping for joy at their deliverance from hunger. . . .

Everything has been done that could be for their relief. Capt. Smith started 4 wagons supplied with food and clothing, and they will soon arrive in our midst, when they will receive all the attention their wants require.[3]

The people in California were presented a somewhat wilder version of the rescue, with remarks of the Army's role in the emigrant catastrophe:

THE SUFFERING IMMIGRANTS NORTH.—A correspondent of the Portland *Advertiser*, writing from the Dalles, November 5th, gives some further particulars of the sufferings of the immigrants who were plundered and reported massacred on Burnt river:

"They were entirely nude, having been stripped of every particle of clothing by the Indians, and when found were subsisting upon the dead bodies of those who had either been killed by the Indians, or died from starvation. When found they were unable to give any account, more than a blank muttering, and starvation had made such havoc that the sad spectacle drew tears from the rough but pitying eyes of the soldiers. The rescued were, four men, two women and six children—twelve in all. Famine and exposure had reduced them to skeletons; some of them were unable to stand, whether overjoyed at relief, or the agonies of their former sufferings overcame them, I know not, but the entire party were raving mad, and as yet can give no account of the rest who composed the train; perhaps other parties are also in the same condition. The work of rescue, however, goes on; everything is done to soothe and save. Captain Dent is nobly doing everything that can be done. The rescued may be in at Walla Walla on or about the 10th. Every means will be employed to discover if any more are to be found. It would seem that robbery alone prompted the Indians; if so, we may yet recover others, who are scattering, perhaps. We will have some explanation from those in high command, in reference to Major Greer and his expedition. Let every one have his just reward. It is evident something was wrong, or Captain Dent would not be sent out at this late day, in the very face of Winter."[4]

Indian Agent Abbott later wrote of his meeting with the survivors of the Utter disaster:

I saw these people at the camp of Captain Dent at the western base of the Blue Mountains on the Umatilla reservation on his return with them, and although he had traveled very slowly and carefully, after resting with them for about a week at their camp on the Owyhee, a more pitiful sight it would be exceeding difficult to imagine. With the exception of Mrs. Myers and the young boys [Munson and Chaffee] who had remained on Burnt river, there was no one in the party who appeared to have the intelligence or mental strength of a child of three years of age. Captain Dent conveyed them to Walla Walla, where they were well supplied and cared for until they recovered normal strength. They were then permitted and assisted to proceed on their way to the Willamette valley.

The facts herein related of the sufferings of the Otter party of immigrants were the worst and most distressing, taken in all their details, of anything that ever came to the knowlege of the author during his many experiences among the Indians in the early days of Oregon.[5]

Abbott's and Captain Smith's letters of the end of October were included a few days later in the 7 November report of the Oregon Superintendent of Indian Affairs to the Commissioner of Indian Affairs in Washington, DC. These and other records were forwarded to the 36th Congress:

It is at length in my power to communicate authentic information in regard to the heart-rending tragedy of the ninth of September, to which I referred in my letter to your office of the 4 ult. This terrible disaster occurred about fifty miles below Salmon Falls on the Immigrant route to Oregon. The company consisted of forty-four persons—seventeen men and twenty-seven women and children—of whom fifteen, after privations seldom paralelled in the annals of human sufferings, are known to survive and have been rescued.

Of the others, the larger number are known to have fallen in their gallant defense, which lasted for thirty-four hours, against an overwhelming force, or in their efforts to escape when compelled to abandon the protection afforded by their wagons. Two men were overtaken and slain near the head of John Day's river. If any of the missing still survive, it is feared they are in captivity to the most cruel and brutal monsters that wear the human form, and are enduring indignities and tortures from which death would be a most welcome refuge.

The names of the survivors are Snyder a discharged soldier who succeeded in reaching the camp of Mr. Cole, as stated in my former letter, Jacob and

Joseph Keith, who found their way to the Umatilla Agency and Mr Munson, Mr Jeffery, Joseph Myers, wife and five children, Mrs Chase (wife of Daniel Chase) and one child and Miss Trimble—twelve persons—rescued by the command of Capt Dent of Army.

Except for Chaffee's name (Jeffery), the Commissioner of Indian Affairs was passing to Congress factual information of the massacre and its aftermath. Perhaps the young army deserter aided in the confusion surrounding his name. The Commissioner:

Capt Dent found those whom he had the good fortune to rescue in the most forlorn condition. They were in a state of perfect nudity, having been stripped by the savages and left to perish. For ten days they had subsisted on the bodies of the dead. When discovered on the 27th of October near the bank of a small stream, they were in a state of extreme emanciation (sic.), their bones almost protruding from their skin. On seeing their deliverers the women and children fell on their knees, and in the most pitious accents implored food. But I will not pain you by attempting a further recital of sufferings, not to be imagined by any who had not been overtaken by a similar calamity. A thrill of horror and of the deepest sympathy vibrates through the whole country, and the universal voice demands that the protection of the government be no longer withheld from our citizens in a district so often and so deeply stained with the blood of the emigrant.

This terrible affair has occurred not far from the horrible massacre of the Wards and their party in the autumn of 1854, a detailed account of which as well as of other outrages by the same savage perpetrators, will be found in the correspondence of this office, on the files of the Indian Bureau.

It is now demonstrated that no adequate protection can be given to the Immigration to this coast, short of the establishment of one or more military posts in the heart of the Snake Country, at points whence the routes of travel, can be constantly guarded, and the several wintering places of the Indians driven by the snows from the mountains, can be readily reached. These Indians should not be permitted to escape punishment for their past cruelties, and must be taught to respect our power, which they now hold in contempt.

I have no doubt that the importance and necessity of adequate military protection to the Immigrant routes to Oregon & Washington will be strongly urged by the present head of this military Department, and that the energetic efforts of the Indian Office will be directed to the attainment of the same object. Without it, immigration by land to this country from the Atlantic States will virtually cease, every enterprise tending to its development languish and untold losses, social, moral and commercial, result.[6]

On the same day the Army also was forwarding news of the emigrant rescue through its channels. Colonel Wright had

the honor to report to the Lieutenant General Commanding-in-Chief, that I have received a communication this day, from Captain Dent, commanding the relief expedition into the Snake Country, reported in my letter to you of the 10th of October. The expedition has been fortunate enough to rescue from starvation twelve members of the party of immigrants attacked by the Snake Indians, at the Salmon Falls. They were found on Burnt River in a state of great destitution, and had been compelled latterly to subsist themselves on the dead bodies of their companions. The enclosed copy of Captain Dent's report gives the names of the rescued, and of those who have been killed, accounting for the whole party. Search for the children of Mr. Van ornan supposed to be in the hands of the Snakes, will be made as soon as the season

sufficiently opens. I hope to retake them. Captain
Dent, reports himself in the snows, — but it is believed
he will be in before the severity of the season will occasion any serious inconvenience to his Command.
Upon his return to Fort Walla Walla, and the rendering
of his report in full, I will again report to the Head
Quarters of the Army.

The rescue by this expedition, from a horrible
death, of so considerable number of this unfortunate
party, is a most gratifying result. No further objects it
appears could be attained in the present state of the
season.

I think it proper to add, that the Officers, and families at Fort Walla Walla, promptly forwarded to the
sufferers, an abundance of clothing and other necessaries and comforts.[7]

]   Arrival At Fort Walla Walla   [

The day after returning to Fort Walla Walla, Captain Dent
finished his official report:

Captain Kirkham greatly facilitated our arrival by
sending forage to feed our worn out animals, and wagons to relieve them of their burdens. We arrived at
Fort Walla-Walla at 11 a. m. on the 7th of November,
1860.

To the officers and men of my command, the em-
ployes of the quartermaster's department, and our
guides, my thanks are due for the zeal, skill, energy,
and humanity which they displayed. To *their* zeal,
skill, and energy, I attribute our success, and to *their*
humanity, the fact that we have brought into this post,
alive and safe, the wrecks of fellow beings we found
on the Owyhee and Burnt rivers.

Very respectfully, your obedient servant,
F. DENT,
Captain 9th Infantry, Comm'g Expedition.

A subscription was taken up for these surviving emigrants at the city of Walla Walla and the Fort. This went to provide them with clothing and other necessities. They were taken in by the officer's wives who provided them with fresh clothing and burned what remnants there were of the old. Margaret Myers cried when they burned her old sunbonnet which had been given to her by a grandmother. She thought they should have spared her father's bullet-riddled hat as his descendents would have prized it.[8]

When the survivors got into Fort Walla Walla a great many people came to see them. Some of the women offered to adopt some of the children. Mrs. Myers could not decide which of her children she could spare, so did not give any away, although Isabella Myers thought Mrs. Chase gave her little Mary to one of the women.[1M]

Mr. A. B. Roberts was one of the many who were eager to hear the survivors' story. "Upon the arrival of the young men here I went at once to see them at their camp at the garrison and while talking with one of the women one of those two young men joined us. The woman would hardly speak to him, but sneeringly said: 'Yes, you skipped out over the hill and left us.' The young man took a walk."[9]

Perhaps the remark was directed at Chaffee. If it was directed at one of the Reith brothers then an explanation for this could be found in the bitter opinion the surviving families held of those who had fled the wagon train, just before it was abandoned. They did not know but that the six who decamped down the trail had all gone together. Margaret wrote of this and of the family's hope for rescue while encamped on the Owyhee:

> To explain the hope they were entertaining, I must go back to the fight. Mr. Van Orman owned two horses, and sometime during the fight, two brothers named Reith, a man named Chaffey, took those horses, mounted them and rode off. Those left fighting were very angry at their desertion, or what seemed to be desertion. Whether they thought it a lost cause

and sought to save their own lives, or whether they hoped to find help we never knew, but incredible as it seems, they escaped the Indians, and after killing one of the horses for food and taking turns riding and walking, they reached Walla Walla, known then as Fort Walla Walla.

Mr. Roberts, and others, heard those rescued "describe the awful occurrence of their disaster and the weary nights that they struggled on carrying helpless children, before they were met by troops sent out to rescue them and how they screamed and wept for joy when they saw the soldiers coming."[10] People wanted to know how the disaster came about and Emeline explained:

Perhaps some of my readers will wonder why we ventured [into] so much danger with so small a train. The reason is we did not intend to cross those dangerous plains alone. We fully expected to overtake a train that was a short distance ahead which got through all right except the one man above mentioned, who left the train to go after some strayed sheep, and was then killed by the Indians. Having failed to overtake them we were left to our fate in spite of all we could do.

There was one family which I cannot forbear to make special mention of, and that is the family of Mr. Joseph Myers. . . . There were seven in the family: father, mother, and five children, and strange as it may seem every one of them were spared, and reached the fort safely. Mr. Myers, in answer to the question asked him how they all happened to get through, when other families were entirely annihilated, answered, "It was prayer saved my family." But I can say that my idea is that extreme selfishness had more to do with their being saved than prayer. Perhaps the good Lord, who is the searcher of all hearts, heeded his selfish prayers, but I would quicker believe that shirking duty and stealing from others was what saved the Myers family.

In addition to famine, the children who starved to death on the Owyhee suffered the emotional and psychological blow of the death of a parent: Abagel and Elijah Utter, or Daniel Chase, Sr. This would impact the children's 'will to live' in their dire circumstances. The Myers children, so close to death when rescued, at least did not suffer that blow: the loss of a parent.

] The Myers Complete Their Journey [

After the Reith brothers brought word of the survivors, a message had been sent to Joseph Myers' brother, Michael, who owned a grocery store in Salem. Michael Myers came up the Columbia to meet his relatives, but did not get to Walla Walla in time to go out with the Army relief force.

Joseph Myers and his family waited a couple of days at Walla Walla before continuing their journey. They went with Joseph's brother, Michael, heading for the brother's home in Salem. Mr. L. W. Coe tendered them free passage by steamboat from Wallula, at the mouth of the Walla Walla River, down the Columbia River. While on the steamboat they were interviewed by Len, the correspondent for the *Oregon City Argus*. Len's letter to his paper was dated the 10th, Saturday.[M] The Myers family arrived at The Dalles Sunday night. A subscription was immediately taken up for them, a portion of which was sent to the sufferers at Walla Walla. The Myers stayed at the Umatilla House, free of charge, where every attention was paid to them by the "gentlemanly proprietors". There, the Dalles correspondent of the *Portland Advertiser* also obtained the Myers' story. In his article, which appeared on Monday, the correspondent stated that the Myers "will arrive in Portland tonight. Mrs. Chase, child and Miss Otter, and two others, whose names I have not learned waited at Walla

Walla."[11] The Myers did go on to Portland, where they arrived Monday night, 12 November. They stopped at the Columbian House hotel. There, Governor Gibbs came to see them. He took Isabella and Margaret to his home for dinner where they told of their experiences.

Versions of the Myers' account of the massacre soon appeared in the Oregon City, Portland, and Salem newspapers. These articles were reprinted in other area newspapers, in Washington Territory, California, and in the *New York Times*. In these versions of the Utter massacre it was reported that the wagon train was first attacked on the 8th of September instead of the 9th. The Myers brought out that the "saved were not, as has been represented, entirely without clothes, but they were but scantily dressed."[M] It was reported that Joseph Myers heard it said that Henry Snyder had plenty of cash when he got in. Myers also commented that he thought Snyder had coin but that he had not cashed his Army check.[M]

California people read an account extracted from the *Portland News* of 14 November. In this interview the deceased John W. Myers was confused with his brother, Joseph.

THE   UNFORTUNATE   IMMIGRANTS.—We yesterday afternoon had a brief conversation with J. W. Myers, [Joseph] leader of the unfortunate train of immigrants. He informs us that there were forty-four in the train at the time of the attack, all, with the exception of one Illinois family, from the State of Wisconsin. Eleven persons were killed outright by the Indians, and only fifteen are known to be survivors of the privations that followed. Myers is firmly of the opinion that if six men had not cowardly deserted them in the first hour of danger, the train would have been able to have driven back the Indians and defended itself through to the settlements. The foremost of the weak-kneed six was the man Snyder, of whose arrival at the Dalles we gave an account some three weeks ago. Only three of these despicable wretches got through to the settlements, and two of them are so

ashamed of their conduct that they keep *incognito*.
With the exception of a brother, Joseph Myers, [John]
who leaves a wife and eight children in Geneva, Wisconsin, to mourn his loss, Myers lost no relatives,
though he brought a large family through with him.
Two girls aged, respectively, eleven and fourteen—
Myers believes to be alive and held in captivity by the
Indians, and thinks that proper exertions might lead to
their recovery. Still suffering exhaustion, and unable
to speak with ease, we received but few particulars
from him.[12]

The Myers' loss in property, due to the massacre, was
over $2,000. The Van Ornum's loss, in money and property,
was about $6,000. They were entirely destitute. Having lost
everything they possessed, the *Portland Advertiser* appealed on
the Myers' behalf to the generosity of the citizens of Portland,
and suggested a general subscription for their relief. The sug-
gestion was acted upon. Liberal contributions were made in
aid of the Myers. The ladies of Portland did much in furnish-
ing the Myers family with clothing. Messrs. G. C. Robbins
and P. J. Holmes collected $540 for the sufferers, including
those remaining at Walla Walla.[13]
The Myers were in Portland for several days. They went
on and settled at Salem. Five more children were born to the
family. Isabella attended Willamette University. She married
William W. Martin who she had first met: "at Galena, Ill.,
where U. S. Grant was then living. That was in the spring of
1860. We were passing through in our prairie schooners on
our way to Oregon. Will was a clerk in a store, and he brought
out a bag of candy for us children." Will came to Oregon later
and married Isabella in 1869; they made their home in Salem.[14]
Margaret Myers finished her story:

The Myers family found their home in the land of father's dreams. The people were all very kind to us on
our arrival in Salem. Mother was urged many times to

write her story for publication, but she told it so many times in the six months that she grew morbind. She was a young woman, only twenty-eight years old, had parted with parents who were growing old; her two brothers whom she never hoped to see again, nor did she; all her young friends of her youth; had seen her little children dying by degrees before her eyes, and her heart was too full to think of ought else at that time. So bitter was her experience that after living more than sixty-two years in Oregon she never loved it or claimed it as her home. Always in speaking of the east, she said "back home."

The little story is done. Some things will seem strange, perhaps, to those reading it. It is written from childish memories and the oft heard story from father's and mother's lips. They have passed on. I cannot consult them as to dates and localities, so let it stand as written.

                                    Margaret Myers Beers.
Salem, Ore., April 11, 1927.

]   At Walla Walla   [

The *Port Townsend North-West* reported that: "among the sufferers who remained at Walla Walla, and were there at last accounts, was Mrs. Chase and child, who is said to have a brother named John Pierce living on Puget Sound. Should this meet the eye of said John Pierce, he is desired to communicate immediately with Mrs. Chase, at Walla Walla."[14] Mrs. Chase is said to have become infatuated with one of the soldiers who had rescued her, a trooper named Frost, and later married him, remaining at Walla Walla.[15]

Emeline Trimble stayed with the family of Lieutenant R. H. Anderson (who she identified as A. J. Anderson)

until my cousin came for me from Salem, Oregon. It was the Lieutenant that rescued us at Owyhee River near old Fort Boysee. They were very kind to me. Mrs. Chase and her little girl stayed at the home of Captain Dent. He was the brother-in-law of Ulysses S. Grant and Captain of the Infantry. They were there when I left.

It was now the middle of December, 1860. Cousin took me to his sister's who had married Mr. J. Pomeroy. My cousin's father, Edward Trimble, was killed on the plains in 1846 by the Indians.* From Salem I went to Linn County, Oregon to my only relative in Oregon that I had ever seen before, Uncle Pierce H. Trimble. . . . They were very kind people, in fact all I met with in the west were kind to me and often tried to help me to forget my troubles. I shall always hold in grateful remembrance the kindness of the people in Washington Territory and Oregon. . . . My schooling did not cost me nor my uncle one cent as the people paid for it. Neither did their kindness stop here. They often came and took me along to entertainments that were going on in the country. The best horse and saddle were always provided me. They wanted me to learn to ride on horseback as that was their mode of traveling there. I soon learned to ride, and often went with the young people to church and singing school. Sometimes eight or ten couples of us went together.

The country was beautiful to ride over, and the scenery was lovely to look at. When the snow was three or four feet deep in Wisconsin, I picked wild flowers in Oregon. Everything around me, so far as nature was concerned was charming to behold. If mother, father, brothers, and sisters had only been with me my joy would have been complete, but they were gone and with all that beauty spread before me, I could not help but turn my longing heart toward them and weep in my loneliness.

---

*See Appendix I, p. 175.

While in the school room trying hard to learn, the scenes of the past would come up before me and it seemed that my heart would break. Nobody knew how hard it was. Many times I was happy with my young friends, and tried to be so; but night would come on and I would pray for dear mother to come take me, and cry myself to sleep. My feet were so injured from walking after the fight, having no shoes and from the cold, I could not always walk to school. Then I rode horseback and picketed out my horse till I returned home. I still suffer much pain in my feet.

The *Oregonian*, 22 December 1860, noted Emeline's passage through Portland. The error of early reports of the massacre persisted: confusing Salmon Falls (on the Snake River) with Salmon River:

Miss Trimble, one of the survivors of the Salmon River massacre, has passed through here on her way to her uncle's in Linn county, under the protection of her cousin.[16]

Chaffee, the young bugler of Company E, 2nd Dragoons, who had deserted from the Portneuf camp, later gave himself up at Fort Walla Walla. The Army records listed him as apprehended in 1861; died 12 March 1862.[17]

One of the Reith brothers died five years after the disaster that befell the Utter train. This would be Joseph, who lost his health as a result of the hardships he had endured.[18]

Just to the west of Pendleton, on the Umatilla River, is Rieth, Oregon. Later, when the Union Pacific Railroad constructed shops and terminals there, the station was named "Rieth" after a family of pioneer settlers who owned land nearby, but, the postal authorities named the post office "Reith." The post office name was later changed as local opinion favored "Rieth," after Louis Rieth, one of two brothers who owned the land where the town now stands. In 1862, two years after Jacob and Joseph Reith crossed the plains, Louis and his brother, Eugene Rieth, also crossed to Oregon. Like Jacob, Louis was born in France, in Alsace-Lorraine in 1846 and accompanied his parents to the United States in 1849. He too lived in Minnesota, having immigrated there with his parents.[19]

Jacob Reith had remained in the area. After recovering from the ordeal of the Utter Disaster he joined the gold rush to the Nez Perce mines at Oro Fino (Idaho). He then went to the mines at Auburn (near where Baker City, Oregon was later located) and toward the end of 1863 had money. He located a ranch on Birch Creek which empties into the Umatilla at Rieth, and he was the first to introduce sheep in that section.

The 1870 Federal Census listed Jacob Rieth, a farmer, aged thirty, as living in "Dwelling 51" of the "Pendleton to Willow Creek" Precinct in Umatilla County, Oregon. On the adjacent line, in "Dwelling 50," was listed four more Rieths: Eugene, twenty-seven, and Louis, twenty-four, were farmers; Mary L., twenty-five, and Julia, eighteen, were keeping house. Also in Dwelling 50 was Catherine Lacknior, age forty-eight, a domestic servant. All were born in France except Julia who was born in New York. The Rieths' name was all spelled the same.

Jacob was still to suffer at the hands of the Indians, in the Bannock Indian War of 1878:

During the raid of the Bannacks, he suffered the loss of some three thousand of his animals. His brother, his partner, narrowly escaped being overtaken, and dissuaded him from venturing out to do what he could to save the flocks. In 1881 he turned his attention chiefly to wheat-raising. . . .
Mr. Reith was married in 1879 to Miss Magdalen Mark[20]

In the 1880 Census of the Pendleton Precinct of Umatilla County, Jacob Reith, age forty-two, was listed with his young wife, Magdalene, and two-month-old daughter, Marie J. Next listed was Louis Reith, a stockman. And in the listing after that was Eugene Reith, wife Helen, and young daughters, Mary C. and Catherine. All last names were spelled the same, but this time were spelled "Reith." Jacob must have had a son soon after this because in the fall of 1958, a Mr. J. L. Reith, age seventy-eight, visited the Owyhee River crossing and the area of the starvation camp. He was a son of one of the Reith brothers who underwent the Utter Disaster.[21]

Fort Boise

TEN

Van Ornum Captives

It was supposed the Van Ornum children were prisoners among some of the Shoshoni in the Snake country. As Indian captives, it was thought that they could yet be alive. Uncle Zacheus never gave up hope of finding his nieces and nephew. Zacheus Van Ornum was a six-foot, black-haired, black-eyed, dark complexioned man from the mining camps of Oregon and California. He had served in the Oregon Mounted Volunteers in the Rogue River War of 1855-56.[1] To this veteran of the Indian uprising, effecting the release of the captive children was a very personal matter. He kept persisting in his efforts.

Others—the Army, Indian Affairs, and private citizens—continued to work for the captives' rescue, and there was good reason to hope for the Van Ornum children's release. The Walla Walla correspondent of the *Portland Times*, wrote on 10 December 1860, that:

> The most important item is the fact that there is a prospect for some more of those unfortunate emigrants to be rescued.
>
> "Eagle of the light," a Nez Perce has just returned from the Snake country and there came with him four Snake Indians who informed the Indian Agent, Mr. Cain, that they knew of four children, members of that unfortunate party, that were yet alive. Arrangements were made with them by which they agree to bring them in and accordingly left their squaws and returned to their country for that purpose. We are in hopes they may succeed.

The prospects for the mines in the Nez Perce country is very flattering. Some difficulty was apprehended with the Indians but I am in the hopes that nothing serious will occur until the government may make some arrangement with the tribe so as to allow those mines to be worked.

We have about four inches of snow in the valley, that fell on the 8th of this month though the weather is clear and pleasant, and stock of every kind is doing well. Wishing you success I remain in haste,

METAT KUES.[2]

The wish for success? Vol. I, No. 1 of the *Portland Times* was published on 19 December. Also in this first issue, there was speculation as to the treatment that the captive children could expect:

Our correspondent from Walla Walla makes known to us the prospect of receiving the captive children among the Snake Indians. The news of their being alive is cheering, and ought to inspire the heart of every citizen to respond to every effort suggested to effect their rescue, If they are compelled to remain among the Indians during the winter, their sufferings will doubtless be severe aside from the liability of the Indians to kill them in case they get short of food. If they expect to treat for a ransom in exchange for them, they may support and protect them for that purpose. But most probably they do not await a ransom. The Snakes have not been known to detain prisoners for a ransom. They are too much separated into small bands without government and system. They will either *murder* or *protect* according to the caprice of the moment. The Indians who reported among the Nez Perces the fact of there being four white children detained among the Snakes, corroborates the suspicion that the Van Norman children were not killed but detained alive. The eagernous with which they left their own women among the Nez Perces, and embraced the opportunity offered them to effect a rescue of their captives makes it quite probable that they may effect their recovery soon to the joy of every sympathetic heart.

With this intelligence before them, we apprehend that the Military of Walla Walla will not leave any means untried for their speedy rescue. The sentiment of both officers and men in the expedition which discovered and rescued the Myers family and those with them, was deeply outraged by the scenes which they witnessed and they are eager to visit punishment upon the ruthless hands which divastated [*sic*] that company of men, women and children. All they want is the order to go, and the order will soon follow the discovery of the mere chance of their rescue.[3]

Three days later the *Oregonian* of 22 December commented on this information:

SUMMARY OF NEWS

We do not learn of the movement of troops at Walla Walla to rescue the children who are prisoners with the Snake Indians. . . . A correspondent of the *Times* at Walla Walla writes: "a Nez Perce Indian has just arrived from the Snake country, with four Snake Indians, who state that there are four white children prisoners with the Snakes. They returned for the purpose of bringing them in." . . . The military expedition against the miners on the Nez Perce reservation, have returned without making an attack upon them. Wiser counsels prevailed. . . . Miss Trimble, one of the survivors of the Salmon River massacre, has passed through here on her way to her uncle's in Linn county, under the protection of her cousin. . . . There is no trouble with the Indians at the Warm Springs reservation, and fears of Indian troubles east of the Cascades have ceased.[4]

Even as the disaster of the Utter and Van Ornum massacres had unfolded, miners led by Elias D. Pierce discovered gold on a tributary of the Clearwater. Under the Treaty of 1855, the peaceful Nez Perce tribes resided on an extensive reservation that encompassed their lands. These lands included areas of the Clearwater and Salmon watersheds and spanned the great gorge of the Snake River which would later be called Hells Canyon.

As the new year began, Colonel Wright and the Governor of Oregon, John Whiteaker, were comparing plans for the captives' rescue. On 3 January Colonel Wright acknowledged

the receipt of your communication of December 28, with respect to Mr. Thompsons proposed expedition into the Snake country and the rescue of the four children said to be in the hands of the Snakes. The subject of the investigation of the truth of the report with regard to these children and of their rescue, if they be in captivity, had from the first moment of the receipt of the intelligence attracted my warmest interest. Messengers dispatched by Major Steen, commanding the troops at Fort Walla Walla, and Mr. Cain, the Indian agent in that neighborhood, have been sent into the Snake country to ascertain if there be any children captives there. These messengers being Nez Perce Indians, known to the Snakes, will not excite their suspicion, and being a small party and acquainted with the country, and not likely to encounter the hostility of the Snakes, they will probably be able to penetrate to the remote locations of the Snakes at this time, notwithstanding the rigor of the season. If the children be alive, they are, if possible, to obtain them by negotiation forthwith. At all events, they are to return and report the information acquired without delay. I have received no report of the return of this party, but hope to hear in a few days. Major Steen, an officer of high reputation for his knowledge of Indians and Indian warfare, and who has spent many years on the frontier

and in campaigns in the Indian country, may be safely
relied upon to achieve all that can be accomplished at
this time.[5]

Continuing the letter, the Governor was informed by Colonel Wright that on 18 December instructions had been sent to
Major Steen to

persevere in the search for the children, and to use all
the means in his power for their rescue. I shall not fail
to take any other steps that may seem necessary to secure this end. That the troops at Fort Walla Walla are
to be relied on for any service that duty and sympathy
for suffering call for is sufficiently evinced by their
late successful expedition immediately after the receipt
of the news of the massacre, the result of which was
the rescue from death of twelve human beings. The
necessity of bringing these helpless sufferers as soon
as possible into the settlements prevented Captain Dent
from prosecuting at the time further search and punishing the Snakes as far as practicable, although when he
started on his return to Walla Walla he was amid the
snows. An energetic campaign against the Snakes, to
be commenced early and continued late, has been, as
you have been informed, determined upon. The matter has been made the subject of correspondence with
the authorities of at the East. It is hoped that the necessary appropriations for the object and for the post at
Boise will be made early. It is not seen that any useful
result can be obtained by the proposed expedition of
Mr. Thompson with twenty-five men. You may rest
assured that whatever can be done for the rescue of the
children will be done by Major Steen. What he proves
himself unable to achieve I doubt if others will be better able to accomplish as the circumstances now are.

The Nez Perces were having to contend with a white
invasion as a stampede of goldseekers poured onto the Nez

Perce reservation. A steamboat plying the Upper Columbia River, the *Idaho*, carried many miners to the confluence of the Clearwater and Snake Rivers, where the town of Lewiston sprang up at the jumping off point for the Nez Perce Mines.

Mr. A. J. Cain, the Indian Agent for the Nez Perce, wrote to the Oregon Superintendent of Indian Affairs about the Van Ornum captives and about problems with the miners:

> Ind Agt. office
> Walla Walla Valley W. T.
> May 1st, 1861,
> . . . . Before leaving the Reservation I heard of the four Van Orman children and dispatched the two Snakes, retaining their wives as hostages for them with an arrangement to meet the parties in June on the South side of the Reservation. The children are reported in the hands of the Snakes called _____ who resort to the Snake river fisheries near "Fort Boise" at this season of the year. I also dispatched messengers to the "Buffalow Nez Percys" in the "Bitter Root Valley" to return home and receive their annuities. I fear if they are left uncontrolled they will make war when the snow entirely disappears from the Mountains.
> Capt. Smith left for the Reservation two days since with one company of Dragoons—his mission will [suffice] for the present.
> The expenditure of so large amount of the money appropriated for the Nez Percy Resa. for foods and the absolute necessity of a disregard of minor considerations of economy in preventing blood shed for months past—has left the service in this part of the country in such a deplorable condition that all its efficiency is lost: and unless the Government speedily remedies matters severe consequences must ensue.[6]

The prospectors fanned out and discovered new finds in the Salmon River Mountains to the south. The rich strike at

Fabulous Florence fueled the full-scale gold rush to the *Idaho Mines*. Getting closer to the scene of the gold rush on the Nez Perce Reservation, Agent Cain attempted to stem the stampede:

Notice

Is hereby given that the settlement made at the junction of Snake and Clear-water rivers is in violation of United States law and cannot be permitted under any circumstances.

The lives of many of our citizens and the immediate prosperity of the country is being greatly endangered by the disregard for Indian rights secured by law. The greatest care and circumspection is now required to maintain peaceful relations with the Indians; And all citizens are earnestly requested to co-operate with the United States authorities to secure this end.

Information has been received of persons passing through the Indian country—telling the Indians there was no government and they should not regard anything said to them by the United States authorities; thereby, inciting them to rebellion: The assistance of all law abiding citizens is earnestly solicited in ascertaining the names of the offenders that they may be dealt with as the law requires.

"Lapwai" Nez Perces Rest.   A. J. Cain
July 7, 1861,   Indian Agent W. T.[7]

The secession of the Southern States led to extensive resignations in the Army as officers and enlisted soldiers left for their homes in the Confederacy. Army regiments were called to the East. Fort Crittenden was closed. Units of the 4th Artillery, 10th Infantry, and 2nd Dragoons under Colonel Cooke departed the former Camp Floyd on 24 July. The troops avoided Salt Lake City and marched by way of Timpanagos Canyon and on past Fort Bridger.[8] The 1st and 2nd Dragoon regiments were redesignated the 1st and 2nd Cavalry. President Lincoln's call for volunteers led to state governments raising and equipping their own army regiments as part of the Union Army. The Oregon Volunteers and California Volunteers were organized, comprised mainly of citizen soldiers.

Agent Cain sent to the Oregon Superintendent of Indian Affairs a copy of the above notice to the miners, and explained the action he had taken:

>   "Lapwai" Nez Perces Reservation
>   July 9, 1861,
>
> Sir:
>   The enclosed copy of notice will explain my action in regard to the settlement at the mouth of the Clearwater. The preservation of peace with the Nez Perces depends upon the effeciency of the Indian service. The council for the distribution of Annuities will meet next week. The principal Chiefs of the tribe directed their people not to go to the "Weipe" root grounds this year, fearing a collision with the miners; this will deprive them of part of their subsistence and I will be compelled to assist them some with provisions if they are to be had, of which I have not received positive information.
>   One of the Snake, I dispatched for information of the Vanorman children captured by that tribe, has returned and reports: the children murdered last fall: the Chiefs quarrelled about the possession of the little girl and then killed them a short distance from the scene of the masacre [sic]. This man also reports all the Snakes in 'Council' near Salmon falls and that some are for war, and some for peace, and say they heard a great many whites were coming across the plains this year who wanted to buy half of their lands, and that the Mormons expected a great many people to join them this year; that "Eagle from the Light" (Nez Perces Chief) was at fort Boise awaiting the result of this council; that "Shap-shese" (Snake)—who was captured when a boy and raised by the Cayuse, and was compelled to flee to the Snake country on account of

depredations in this country is counseling for war; and that the Snakes and the Mormons are to have an understanding soon.

Of the hostility of all the Snakes there is no doubt; and I have long since been satisfied that "Eagle from the Light" was, on the part of the hostile Nez Perces, endeavoring to form a combination with other tribes for a war against the government; he was in the Snake country last year about the time of the emigrant massacre and the reports of his being killed by the Snakes were only circulated to conceal his designs. The Mormons have for a long time exercised an improper influence over the minds of the Indians with whom they have intercourse, and I am firmly convinced, they are now taking advantage of our national troubles to incite a general Indian war. It is of the highest importance that peaceful relations should be preserved with the Nez Perces to prevent the entire success of these machinations.

The immediate interest of Oregon and Washington are dependant upon the development of the interior country and the overland routes, and as the people have always been too prone to lay all their misfortunes at the door of the general government, I regard no sacrifice too great to maintain peace at the present time.

Capt. Smith has rendered very valuable service in preserving quiet on the Reservation.

I have been quite ill for some weeks, but am now recovering my usual health.[9]

The emigration of 1861 could attest to the 'hostility' of the Snakes, as there were several encounters with Indians along the Snake river. A. B. Roberts experienced this threat when he made a fearful trip into the Snake country to meet relatives who were to join him at Walla Walla. (He visited the grounds of both the Van Ornum and Utter massacres.) The Harriman wagon train was attacked on 8 August 1861 at City of Rocks in the same area where another train had been taken the previous year (7 September 1860, just two days before the Utter Train was attacked).* In this milieu, efforts to rescue the Van Ornum captives came to naught.

]   Missing Van Ornums   [

The fall of 1861 found Elias D. Pierce in Walla Walla. His knowledge of the Clearwater country had been gained through several trading trips among the Nez Perces. He had used that knowledge the previous fall in circumventing the Nez Perce warriors that guarded their trails. Pierce had surreptitiously led the party of miners along the Clearwater where they discovered the gold on Oro Fino Creek that launched the Idaho gold rush. This past summer (1861) he had been to the Snake river plains, and now proposed another trading expedition into the Snake Country with the possibility of rescuing the Van Ornum captives. To that end he had written Henri M. Chase who had traversed the Snake Country, also that summer. Chase replied:

> WALLA WALLA, Nov. 1st, 1861.
> CAPT. PEARCE,—*Dear Sir*: Yours of Oct. 21st, asking information concerning the children who are now captives among a band of the Snake indians came to hand and I have to say in answer that I will cheerfully give all the information which I possess on the subject. The children in question were taken from the party of emigrants who were massacred on Snake River about eighty miles below the Salmon Falls in the Fall of 1860, and belong to the family of Van Norman There was no certain information gained as to their fate until I reached Salt Lake City in May last, at which time I called upon Col. B. Davies, the Sup't of Indian Affairs for Utah; who by special appointment authorized me to use all means in my power to collect information concerning them and if possible to recover

---

*See Appendix II, "Wagon Train Taken at City of Rocks, 1860," Appendix III, "A. B. Roberts Visits Utter Massacre Sites," and Appendix IV, "1861 Attack on the Harriman Train."

them from their captors. I employed Mr. A.
Huntington of Salt Lake who has been a long resident
of the Snake country and speaks the language of that
tribe fluently. He proceeded at once to the Indian
country when he learned beyond a doubt that the children were held by the Goose Creek Indians, and
passed the proceeding winter in the Thousand Spring
Valley. I also had "talks" in the presence of Col.
Davies with the principal men of the tribes of Southern
Oregon and Northern Utah, who all confirmed this
statement. I now made preparations for a journey
among the Indians, expecting to get an escort from
Fort Crittenden, but the troops were all ordered east. I
now took the field with three men which was all that I
was able to procure owing to the dangerous nature of
the trip. I soon found that this party was too small, so
I proceeded down Snake River towards this section of
country. I saw a number of Snakes on the route with
whom I talked and made some presents and endeavor-
ed to prevail upon them to desist from their murderous
practices upon travelers, which they promised to do,
saying that this "talk" was new to them. This is a brief
sketch of my operations in the Snake country. Now,
sir, my opinion based upon a twelve years experience
of indian character is, that the best and only way to recover the captive children is to enter the field early in
the spring with a force of not less than fifty experienced men, and to take a quantity of indian goods and
with these goods to ransom or purchase them from the
Indians. It would require, however, a man of sagaci-
ty, and intimate knowledge of Indian character to head
the expedition. I am strongly in hopes that you will
undertake this yourself and I would then be sure of the
result. It is only necessary for some man of known
experience to take the lead in this matter, and crowds
of ready hearts and hands would soon flock to his
standard. Owing to the unsettled state of affairs East it

is not probable that any U. S. force could be spared
for this undertaking. But it would be better for any
one taking this matter in hand to have special authority
from the Commissioner of Indians Affairs, which I
have no doubt could be procured. I forwarded some
time since my reports to his office but as yet received
no communication from the Department.

Henri Chase's response to Pierce's inquiry about the Van
Ornum children prompted a reply. Pierce was again, or still, in
Walla Walla when he wrote on the 23d that

your reply is not only satisfactory to my former confirmed opinion that those children were yet retained by
the Snakes, but, sir, allow me to say that the indefatig-
able exertions on your part to obtain the requisite information relative thereto, does not only gratify and
emulate in me a disposition to use all and every available means to recover them, but, sir, it has been on
your behalf a most praiseworthy and hazardous undertaking that will meet with a hearty response from every
heart that possesses magnanimity to feel for suffering
humanity, and is entitled to an eulogy that I shall not
offer to give. Now, sir, in answer to your request that
I should undertake the laudable expedition of recaptur-
ing those unfortunate children is the highest ambition
to which I would aspire, and I say explicitly I will do
it if I can get a response of an hundred men by the 1st
day of May next. I do not endorse your plan of trading for those children with these natural savages who
massacred their parents and whose blood cries for
vengeance at your and my hands, but will, as policy
may dictate, be governed by circumstances entirely. I
will, in due time, make the necessary call on the citizens of Walla Walla and arrange the plan of operations
so as to make the rendezvous at this place and be ready
to march by the 1st of May as above suggested.

The above two letters were printed in the Walla Walla *Washington Statesman* on 29 November under the heading, "The Captive Children," with the observation that the

> correspondence between Mr. Chase and Capt. Pierce, will be found interesting to readers. The letter of Mr. Chase reveals the horrible condition in which these unfortunate children yet remain, victims to one of the most fiendish tribes of Indian. Our people would assuredly hail their delivery from the hands of these brutal savages with rejoicings. The movement contemplated by Capt. Pierce is a most laudable one, and we trust he may meet with signal success in raising the necessary number of men and equipage for the proposed expedition into the Indian country. We think the expedition could not have been trusted to better hands. The Captain is a determined man, an old mountaineer, and possesses a thorough knowledge of the Indian character.

It is doubtful that this proposed expedition progressed any further. For decades the winter of 1861-62 was the worst or greatest of record on the amount of snowfall in the Pacific Northwest. The following May a group of prospectors came in through the Snake Country and found the Boise River overflowing two miles wide. They managed to cross the flood in the Boise valley and entered the Boise Basin. There—in the mountains just north of where the Oregon Trail struck the Boise River—was discovered the greatest find of placer gold in the Pacific Northwest.

The ensuing stampede of miners led to even more discoveries of minerals. As miners poured into eastern Washington Territory, strikes were made south of the Salmon River. James Warren led a party that found a gold field high in the mountains just to the south of that river. The area became known as *The Warrens*.[10] The horde of miners, so far removed from the seat of territorial government on Puget Sound, demanded the creation of another new mining territory.

The influx of miners into their lands also introduced a new element for the Shoshoni to deal with. This was of concern to the Bureau of Indian Affairs as well, and to the US Army which was undergoing reorganization with state volunteer regiments. In the midst of these tumultuous events, Zacheus Van Ornum persisted in working with the army and the government to bring about the rescue of his brother's children from the Snake Country.

ELEVEN

Fate of the Captives

There was speculation about the Van Ornum children, and rumors. Emeline Trimble recalled:

> Three of the Van Orman girls and one boy had been carried away by the Indians. The next year we heard by some emigrant trains something of them. The oldest girl, 13 years old, was killed. In attempting to get away she killed two squaws, and then the Indians killed her. The boy was bought by an emigrant train and reached his uncle in Oregon. The Indians were seen leading the two little girls with collars around their necks and chains to lead them by. A thousand pities that they had not all been killed with their parents. I have that one consolation, that in all my troubles none of my folks were taken captive by them.[E]

Perhaps a little of what Emeline heard was correct. Almost two years after their capture, it was still not known what became of the Van Ornum children. The Army continued to effect their rescue. A full year of fighting between the warring states resulted in many disruptive changes in the government and military. Benjamin Alvord, a Brigadier-General of US Volunteers, now commanded the District of Oregon, which was still headquartered at Fort Vancouver, Washington Territory. From there, on 8 July 1862 Alvord wrote W. H. Rector, the new Superintendent of Indian Affairs at Salem, Oregon:

Will you please give me any information contained in your office as to what Snake Indians were the murderers of the emigrants near Fort Boise in the autumn of 1860. I desire to instruct the commanding officer of the expedition which will soon leave Fort Walla Walla for the emigrant road for the protection of the emigrants to embrace any opportunity which may occur to apprehend those murderers if their identity can be established. Are you or your neighbors able to inform me where information on the subject can be obtained? If you know of any of that emigrant party who would be a suitable person to be employed in that capacity, I would endeavor to secure his services to accompany said expedition—or, preferably, any one having the most reliable information on the subject. I shall cause inquiries to be made at or near Fort Walla Walla, but apprehend difficulty in obtaining such information as I want.[1]

The Oregon Superintendent of Indian Affairs had not been idle on the captive matter. General Alvord's query was promptly replied to by Mr. Rector, who wrote from Salem on 11 July

that the records of this office do not furnish the information which you desire, or which would materially assist you in your expedition. There is however, residing in this city Mr. Joseph Myers, one of the survivors of that terrible tragedy. I have had a personal interview with Mr. Myers, and he feels confident of his ability to identify some of the Indians engaged in the massacre wherever he should see them. One in particular he describes as being of medium size, rather slim, blind in one eye, with long hair, generally pulled down over the blind eye, with considerable beard, especially on the upper lip; another one of rather low stature and very fleshy. The Indian first described came to their camp on Rock Creek, beyond Salmon Falls, and followed the train until the attack was made, and remained during the entire fight. Mr. Myers and family were present during the entire attack . . .[2]

In discussing the Reith brothers, either Joseph Myers could not recall Joseph Reith's name or the Superintendent of Indian Affairs had gotten it in error. Mr. Rector continued his letter to General Alvord by mentioning Joseph Myers' predicament:

He is well prepared to give you full information on many points, and I am confident would be of great service to the expedition. He expresses a willingness to accompany the military, provided arrangements can be made for the support of his family during his absence. He is in indigent circumstances (having lost his all on that occasion), with a wife and six children to support, five of whom were with him when the outrage was perpetrated. He refers me to two others, young men, Jacob and Samuel Rieth, who are now somewhere in the Salmon River mines. They were also of the party. In connection with this subject I desire to say that an appropriation has been made for negotiating some treaty of friendship with the Snake Indians, and measures are now on foot to secure the Indians' consent to a meeting with an agent of the Government for this purpose. It is my earnest desire as soon as instructions are received from the Department to proceed at once to this work, and if possible prevent any similar occurrence. Should the instructions be received during the time this expedition will remain out I desire to avail myself of their protection. I will start within a week to visit the agencies east of the mountains, and will be pleased to call upon you and have a further interview concerning the matter.

] The Oregon Volunteers [

As the Army prepared its 1862 expedition to the Snake Country, the following notice appeared in the 15 July *Portland Times*:

A CARD!
The Murderers of the Emigrants
in 1860.
Any person having information of a reliable character as to the identity or probable locality of the Snake Indians, who were guilty of the murder near Fort Boise of the emigrants in the autumn of 1860, is requested to give information at the office of the district commander at Fort Vancouver, W. T., or to the commanding officer at Fort Walla Walla.
July 11th, 1862.

The military forces patrolling the Oregon Trail were directed to search for the Indians who attacked the Utter train. Lieutenant Colonel Reuben F. Maury, of the First Oregon Cavalry at Fort Walla Walla, was assigned to command the 'Expedition upon the Emigrant Road, Wash. Ter.' on 15 July. The principal object of the expedition was

the protection of all travelers, and especially of the expected emigration. In general, as you pass through the Indian country it will be proper to make known that your purpose is not to wage war upon any tribe, but to protect the whites. You are also expected, as far as lies in your power, to enforce the Indian intercourse act of the 30th of January, 1834 (see paragraph 517 of Army Regulations), forbidding the introduction and sale of intoxicating liquors among the Indian tribes. If incidentally you should be able to get possession of the Snake Indians engaged in the murder of the emigrants near Fort Boise in the autumn of 1860, and

shall be able in a satisfactory manner to identify the
murderers, the general commanding desires you to
deal with them in a summary manner.   You are
directed to proceed as far as Salmon Falls, on Snake
River, and not to return to Fort Walla Walla before the
1st of November.   You will remain encamped at some
eligible point near Salmon Falls as long as possible,
for that is the principal haunt of the Snake Indians for
the purpose of fishing in the summer time.   He does
not desire you to interfere with their fishing or other
peaceful avocations, and your interpreter may, as you
approach that region, have some opportunity of sending them word to that effect.   In most of the tribes in
this country, the murderers or offenders are known
and acknowledged by the whole tribe without attempt
at concealment.   It may be different with the Snakes.
The general commanding is satisfied that with all the
tribes the surest preventive of future murders is the
arrest and punishment of those guilty of past offenses.
As you advance you may find it advisable to establish
one or two depots of supplies, where you should leave
enough for the return of the command from those
points.   The general commanding desires me to enjoin
upon you the importance of the preservation of order,
and especially that whenever your command comes in
contact with camps of peaceable Indians, the Indians
should be vigilantly protected from injury and violence
from all whites, whether soldiers or citizens.   The general desires to receive reports of your progress from
time to time, sent through the express of Wells, Fargo
& Co., at Walla Walla.   Opportunities may offer of
sending letters by reliable travelers, but you are authorized to send an express yourself whenever you may
deem it of sufficient importance.[3]

The captive Van Ornum children's Uncle Zacheus was relentless in his efforts to recover them.   This summer of 1862
he had concrete news about his nephew.   James H. Martineau

(twenty years later in his "Military History of Cache Valley")
wrote:

> Some of the whites in Cache Valley had seen the child
> with the Indians, and although the latter had painted its
> face to resemble themselves, its light hair and blue
> eyes betrayed its race. The Whites tried to get the
> child, but the Indians refused to let it be ransomed,
> and finally kept it secreted.[4]

In late summer Zacheus was at Walla Walla, seeking to
join the Army expedition into the Snake River country. Colonel Justus Steinberger of the First Washington Territory Infantry commanded Fort Walla Walla. On 11 August he trans-
mitted to District of Oregon Headquarters a

> copy of a letter this day given to Mr. Z. Van Orman
> for Lieutenant-Colonel Maury, in command of the
> emigrant road expedition. A friend and relative of Mr.
> Van Orman has just arrived from the East, and has
> seen the children referred to. He attempted to buy
> them, but was unsuccessful, the Indians refusing to
> give them up except at very great price. Mr. Van
> Orman has arranged to take out with him the person
> alluded to, hoping to overtake Colonel Maury's com-
> mand and secure his aid in the recovery of the chil-
> dren. Convinced that a public service will be secured
> in asking Colonel Maury's assistance to further the
> purpose, and trusting it will meet the approval of the
> commanding general . . .[5]

The enclosed letter of the same date from Steinberger to
Reuben F. Maury, First Oregon Cavalry—en route to Salmon
Falls—stated:

> The bearer of this, Zachias Van Orman, is the brother
> of Alexis Van Orman, who with his wife and oldest
> son was massacred in 1860 by the Upper Bannocks, a

portion of the Snake Indians, near old Fort Boise. He goes out tomorrow to overtake your command with another person familiar with the country in which the murder took place. Four children of Alexis Van Orman were at the time of the massacre taken prisoners by these Indians, and are still in their hands. They have been seen by the person alluded to and are known both to him and the uncle who carries this to you. The sole object that takes out Mr. Van Orman is to recover the children prisoners, and learning of your expedition he has applied to me to enlist your co-operation in his views. Believing that your instructions will permit you to give him assistance in this purpose, I have earnestly to recommend this gentleman to your consideration and your aid in the recovery of the prisoners. Mr. Van Orman in his relationship with these children has much interest in the recovery of them, and will be able to give you valuable information that may lead to this end.[6]

Lieutenant Colonel Maury, commanding the Emigrant Road Expedition,* reported from Camp Bruneau, Snake River, on 22 September that:

Nothing definite has been heard of the Van Orman children. Their uncle. Z. Van Orman, has gone through to Salt Lake City. In this connection I will mention that one Indian at the falls said that it was the Indians who live in the vicinity of Harney Lake who committed the massacre, and that the children were taken prisoners. Since then he had heard nothing of them, but had no doubt they had been killed.[7]

As the Oregon Volunteers operated along the Snake River, an Army volunteer force from the state of California, under the

*As the First Oregon Cavalry came east on the Trail to Salmon Falls, further east there occurred a series of Indian attacks on emigrant trains. Two small trains were attacked on 9 August 1862 in the vicinity of what would later be called Massacre Rocks. This and an ensuing fight with the Indians resulted in the death of ten emigrants. One of two other trains in the area was later attacked at City of Rocks, as were other groups of emigrants.

command of Colonel Patrick Edward Connor, moved east in Utah Territory to solve the Indian depredation problem. The Californians built Fort Ruby in September 1862 and intended to reopen Fort Crittenden (formerly Camp Floyd) which was in the desert forty miles from Salt Lake City. Fort Crittenden was found to be unusable so the California Volunteers built Camp Douglas* on a hill overlooking Salt Lake City .

]   Rescue of Reuben   [

From the newly established Camp Douglas, Colonel Connor sent forth a rescue force. It was apparent in the order that the Colonel assumed the 1860 Van Ornum massacre happened as part of the series of Indian attacks on emigrant trains in 1862:

> HEADQUARTERS DISTRICT OF UTAH,
> Camp Douglas, Utah Ter., November 20, 1862.
> Maj. E. MCGARRY,
> Second Cavalry California Volunteers:
> MAJOR: You will proceed this p.m. with a detachment of sixty men of your command to Cache Valley, at which point are encamped Bear Hunter's tribe of Snake and Bannock Indians, who, I am credibly informed, have in their possession an emigrant boy about ten years of age, whose parents were murdered last summer by Indians. The boy's uncle is at present at Cache Valley and will guide you to where the boy is. You will march by night and by a trail which will be shown you by a guide who will accompany your command. Surround the Indians, if possible, before they become aware of your presence, and hold them prisoners while you send a part of your men to a valley about two miles from the Indian camp, where, I am told, there is a large number of stock stolen from murdered emigrants, which, if you

---

*Camp Douglas was designated a Fort two years later. It was closed in December 1991.

have reason to believe that my information is correct, you will drive to this post. You will search the Indian camp thoroughly for the emigrant boy, and if you should not find him you will demand him of the Indians, and if not given up you will bring three of their principal men to this post as hostages. You will also investigate as to their complicity in the massacres of last summer, and if you have reason to believe any of them are guilty you will bring all such to this post for trial. You will not fire upon the Indians unless you find it necessary to the proper execution of your instructions.[8]

Just three days later David Moore, the Colonel commanding the 5th Regiment, Weber County Militia, along with Major F. A. Hammond, Indian Interpreter George Hill, and Clerk Daniel Gamble wrote Utah Superintendent of Indians Affairs, James D. Doty:

We understand through Indian Tom that a company of Cavalry from Col. Connor's Command are in search of a white child, said to be in Bear Hunters band, (Who are friendly indians and never known to be engaged in plundering Emigrants) From Indian Tom's positive information and other reliable statements their is no white child in that band, but their is a half breed the son of a French Mountaineer—by the sister of cheif WashaKee principal cheif of the Shosho-Nee Nation, Said child is about 15 years old with yellow hair and light complextion cannot talk English, on the approach of the Soldiers the Band fled to the Mountains to avoid colission with them, and sent this Indian as a Messenger of peace.[9]

Perhaps Indian Tom was correct in stating there was a fifteen-year-old half breed boy who could not speak English, but with blond hair? Praben A. Hansen, who was born in Denmark in 1850, as a lad lived at Plain City, between Ogden and

Brigham City, U. T.[10] Hansen later wrote that when he was eleven years of age these Indians had a white boy with them:

> I have wrestled with this boy many a time, and I came to find out that his name was Reuben Smith, and that he was captured by the Indians on the old Oregon Trail out west. The Indians destroyed the entire train except the boy and his little sister, and this girl went north with part of the band and he never heard of her after that. I used to know, old Pocatello well, and all the old Indians. Old Bear Tusk, and all the rest of the tribe in my time. They would come down to Plain City every day during melon time and we had a great time with their kids wrestling and many other kinds of sports.[11]

The *Deseret News* on 26 November 1862, recounted what was known of the Van Ornum captives and events leading to this rescue effort:

EXPEDITION FOR THE RECOVERY OF A CAPTIVE

On last Thursday evening, a detachment of some sixty men belonging to the 2d cavalry Cal. Volunteers, under Major McGarry, left Camp Douglas, by order of Col. Connor, for Cache Valley, the object of the expedition being, as understood, the recovery of a white boy, held as a captive by an Indian, belonging to a band of Shoshones, now encamped, as reported, on the north side of Bear River, not far from Franklin. How long the boy has been a captive, who his parents were, and where and when he was taken by the Indians, we know not; but have been informed that the Indian who now has him in possession, was not his captor; but that he was obtained by purchase or otherwise, from another band, together with a sister younger than he; that after it became known to the people in

Cache county, that the band of Indians who frequently roam through that part of the Territory had two white children in their possession, efforts were made to get them by fair means, if possible; that the little girl, who was sickly, was obtained from the Indian who claimed her, by some person who succeeded in persuading him to part with her, for a pecuniary consideration; but nothing would induce the owner of the boy to give him up to the whites. The little girl subsequently died; and the boy is yet with the Indians, who are said to think highly of him, and value him at twenty ponies.

The Van Ornum girl referred to above would be the youngest child, Lucinda, about eight years old. The white boy was Reuben, now ten years old, who probably was instructed to give his name as Smith. The *Deseret News* continued by describing young Reuben:

The little fellow is represented as being a very active, sprightly lad, about ten years of age, and can speak the Shoshone dialect as well as the English language quite fluently. He is said to remember the massacre of his father and mother by the Indians, somewhere on the plains, who took him, a younger brother and two sisters captives. He says his brother cried a good deal, and that the Indians took him off with them one day, after which, he never saw him again, and does not know what became of him—neither does he know whether the other sister is dead or alive.

The fate of one of the two older Van Ornum girls, either Eliza or Minerva, was here revealed, although the *Deseret News* incorrectly described the girl as being a brother. The article referred to Zacheus Van Ornum and the circumstances leading to the expedition:

Some weeks since, a man from Oregon, whose name has not transpired, claiming to be the boy's uncle, while at Smithfield, saw the lad and conversed with him, and, altho' the Indians were about, was a very good opportunity to take and bring him away, which for some cause, he thought proper not to do, but subsequently made some threats of what he would do, in the event that he could not obtain the custody of the boy, and then came to Salt Lake City and succeeded in getting the detachment of troops sent out to take him from the Indians by force. The result of the expedition will shortly be made known. It is hoped that it will be favorable, but fears are entertained that it will not, and that the life of the boy will be imperiled thereby.

Army records report the result of the 20 to 27 November 1862 "Expedition from Camp Douglas to the Cache Valley" in Utah Territory. Major Edward McGarry commanded the expedition. He left Camp Douglas

on the night of the 20th instant and proceeded to Cache Valley, where I arrived about 11 p.m. on the 22nd, a distance of 100 miles, where I was met by Mr. Van Orman, the uncle of the emigrant boy you ordered me to rescue from the Indians; he informed me that Chief Bear Hunter was encamped with thirty or forty of his tribe, Shoshones, Snakes, and Bannocks, about two miles distant. I left the horses in the settlement called Providence in charge of a guard, and started about 1 o'clock for the Indian camp; the night was dark and cold, and we did not find the camp until the morning of the 23rd. I then divided my command into three parties under Captain Smith, Lieutenant Conrad, and myself, with instructions to surround the camp and close in upon them at daybreak. I found in a tent two squaws; the Indians had all left that night, as I perceived that the fires in their huts were not extinguished. I then returned to where I had left the horses, at which place I arrived about 7 a.m. Captain Smith brought in one Indian, caught in trying to escape; I made a prisoner of him. About 8 o'clock a party of mounted Indians, I should think thirty or forty, armed with rifles, bows and arrows, made their appearance from a canyon on a bench between the settlement and hills, about a mile from the settlement, and made a warlike display, such as shouting, riding in a circle, and all sorts of antics known only to their race. I immediately ordered my men to mount, divided them as before, sent Captain Smith to the right, Lieutenant Conrad to the left, and I took the center, driving the Indians into the canyon; when I arrived at the mouth of the canyon I halted for the purpose of reconnoitering; just at that time the Indians opened fire upon Lieutenant Conrad; I then ordered my men to commence firing and to kill every Indian they could see; by this time the Indians had possession of the canyon and hills on both sides. I found it would be impossible to enter the canyon without exposing my men greatly. I therefore re-enforced Lieutenant Conrad on the left of the canyon, with orders to take the hill on the left of the canyon at all hazards. About the time the re-enforcements reported to him Chief Bear Hunter made his appearance on a hilltop on the right, with a flag of truce (as I was informed afterward); I at the time took it to be a warlike demonstration; a citizen who heard his halloing came up to me and told me that the chief said they did not want to fight any more. I then ordered my men to cease firing, and told him to say to the chief if they would surrender and come in I would not kill them, which terms they acceded to. Chief Bear Hunter, with twenty or more of his warriors, then came in. I took them into the settlement, took Bear Hunter and four others that I thought to be prominent Indians and examined them (through an interpreter) as to the whereabouts of the white boy, and ascertained that he had been sent away some days before. I told Bear Hunter to send some of his tribe and bring the boy to me; that

I should hold the five as hostages until they delivered him to me. He dispatched three of his men, and they returned the next day about noon with the boy. I then released Bear Hunter and the four others. I killed 3 and wounded 1 Indian in the fight. I was told by Bear Hunter that an Indian know as Woeber Tom, alias Utah Tom, communicated the information of our approach. In relation to the emigrant stock I was ordered to examine into and bring into camp, I could not find any such, and from the information I could gather I am of the opinion all or nearly all of the stock taken by the Indians last summer is now in the Humboldt country. I left Cache Valley on the morning of the 25th, and arrived at this camp on the afternoon of the 27th, without the loss or scratch of man or horse. It affords me great pleasure to report to the colonel commanding the good conduct of the command, and during the fight, which lasted about two hours, the officers and men behaved handsomely.[12]

On 2 December the Commander of the District of Utah forwarded McGarry's report to the Department of Pacific Army Headquarters and also disclosed:

The uncle of the boy, who is now at this post, is a resident of Oregon, and, as he informs me, has been in search of the boy for two years. Three sisters of his, who were captured at the same time, are dead. He also informs me that three expeditions had previously been sent out from Oregon for the recovery of the children, one of which was under command of Captain Dent, of the Ninth Infantry. The Indians are threatening the Overland Mail Route east and west of here. I have no fears of the western end, as the lessons I have been teaching them and the messages I send them make them fear me. About a week since I sent ten men to protect the telegraph station at Big Sandy, which was threatened by Indians. On Saturday last they stole 100 horses from Fort Bridger Reserve, belonging to some mountaineers, who are wintering there, and fears are entertained that they will attack some of the stations of the Overland Mail. I have therefore ordered Company I, Captain Lewis, of my regiment, to garrison Fort Bridger this winter. I shall order detachments of his company to the different stations in this district east of here, if I find it will be necessary. Pacific Springs Station, lately attacked by Indians, is just east of the line dividing this district and the Department of the West, and has been garrisoned by troops from that department. The telegraph station at Big Sandy is in the District of Oregon. I shall leave the ten men now there at that point until I am satisfied there is no further danger from Indians, unless otherwise ordered.[13]

The next day the *Deseret News* announced the return of Major McGarry's expedition:

which left Camp Douglas on the evening of the 20th ult., for the purpose of recovering a boy alleged to have been held as a captive by Bear Hunter's band of Indians, encamped in Cache valley, returned with the lad on Thursday last, having been absent one week.

As we were going to press last evening we received from Maj. Blair an account of the affair, which was too late for publication.

It appears that the troops had a fight with the Indians near Providence, lasting about an hour. "Federal loss, none—Red skin the same." The Indians withdrew in "good order," after which the Indians called for peace and delivered up the boy—whom they claim to be a half breed—his father a Frenchman, his mother a sister of Wash-i-kee, the Shoshone chief.

Another account of the rescue of Reuben Van Ornum was given by Henry C. Haskin, in a letter printed in the *Napa County Reporter* on 20 December:

CAMP DOUGLAS, U. T., Nov. 29th, 1862.

. . . The Quarters of our Company are nearly completed, with the exception of those for the Officers, and the Stables are also progressing finely. The Men's Quarters are constructed by excavating the earth five or six feet deep and the size desired, around which log huts are built, and the whole then covered with the tent canvass. The mode of egress is by a covered passage of steps leading down to the interior. The Quarters of the Officers are constructed of adobe walls but with this exception, are like the Men's. The Stables are built of palisades, and covered with brush, the whole receiving a coating of dirt. Forage is coming in at the rate of 150 loads per day; and our produce costs us about California prices. . .

Maj. McGarry, of Napa, in command of the 2d Cavalry, was sent out on the 21st inst., under sealed orders, which afterwards appeared to be the regaining of the nephew of their guide, a white boy about ten years old, who had been in captivity about three years. When the expedition arrived at the point of destination, they found the bird had flown, the Indians thinking thus to elude the Major. McGarry with his command, followed on, and after undergoing great exposure and hardships in wading through ice-cold streams waist deep, subject to the fire of the red devils, succeeded in

---

Eliza Van Ornum	13	Killed or died of starvation 1861
Minerva Van Ornum	probably 12	Died of starvation 1861
Lucinda Van Ornum	6	Rescued by purchase 1862, died
Reuben Van Ornum	8	Rescued November 1862
		(Ages at time taken captive)

Fate of the Captives.   (Complied by Author).

---

capturing the Chief of the tribe and four or five of his
Hi-u-muck-i-mucks. He demanded from them the
production of the captive by noon of the next day, and
if not forthcoming, his captives would be marched to
Camp, where they might expect to receive no gentle
treatment. The threat had its effect and the captive was
duly produced at the time designated. He was dressed
and bedaubed with paint like an Indian, and acted like
a regular little savage when given into our possession,
fighting, kicking and scratching when the paint was
washed from him to determine his white descent. . . .

Col. Connor, commanding this District is a man
well suited to the position, and I believe is highly re-
spected by both Officers and men. I believe the most
of us are better satisfied with a soldier's life than we
were in California, but would be better pleased to
know we were going farther East in the Spring.

Our force at present is nine Companies, four of
Cavalry and five of Infantry, and about seven hundred
and thirty strong. The health of the men has been very
good, with not a death among us since our arrival. We
have a number of Napa Boys among us, and they
promise their friends in that County that they shall
always hear a good account of them, be it in battle or
in Camp.[14]

] Zacheus & Reuben [

Zacheus Van Ornum remained in Utah Territory for a few
months. It was about then that Zacheus and Reuben were pictured in a tintype with eight "frontier scouts and Indian fighters."[15] Zacheus continued to serve as a scout and in January
was present at the Battle of Bear River:

the fall and winter of 1862 and 1863 I was employed
by the quartermaster of Camp Douglas, Utah, commanded by Cornel (Connor) a portion of the time for 5

months and the other part of the time as scout. I was
in too engagement. I was at the Slaughtor on Bear
River. and at the Capturing of my Nephew at Cash
Valley by Major McGerry I was in both engagements

Zacheus returned east and again married. (He had first
married Catherine Coly on 16 January 1849.) The second
marriage was to Elizabeth Rowe on 16 or 17 April 1864 at
"Waldlock" (Waldwick) Town, Iowa County (just north of the
La Fayette County line), Wisconsin. "Afterwards I was
eployed by Cornel Mowery to accompany Lieutenant Hobart
on a raid up Snake River as guide and interpreter," the fall of
1864:[16]

HEADQUARTERS,
Fort Boise,* Idaho Ter., September 17, 1864.
SIR: Letters to the 14th have been received from
Lieutenant Hobart. He was then with the cavalry of
his command at Three Islands, about thirty miles
below Salmon Falls, and was hastening by night
marches to the Upper Bruneau, where he has been informed, through a prisoner captured on the 13th, of a
camp of fifteen or twenty lodges with considerable
stock. On the 13th the lieutenant found and attacked a
considerable camp above the Three Islands, killing
five men and wounding others. They were a party that
had lately stolen some flour, &c., at the crossing of
the Malade River. The flour was found in their camp.
I have heretofore neglected to mention that Lieutenant
Hobart while en route to Salmon Falls met Mr. Z. Van
Orman, the uncle of the Van Orman children, with one
of the children—supposed to be—(he obtained it, I
think, through the Indian agent, Salt Lake, last winter), and employed him as guide and interpreter. His
familiarity with their language, as well as personal

---

*A permanent fort was finally established in the Boise valley in 1863 with Boise City immediately
springing up as a mining supply point at the site of the new Fort Boise.

Zacheus & Reuben Van Ornum
From the tintype taken after Reuben's rescue. (Drawing by Kathleen Petersen, Boise, Idaho)

knowledge of many Indians, makes him of great service. The Indian killed was from the Owyhee. I hope
to hear in a few days the result of Lieutenant Hobart's
visit to the Bruneau. The activity and zeal of Lieutenant Hobart and command deserve credit and commen-
dation. Lieutenant West with most of the infantry had
gone up Snake River expecting to reach the Great Falls

and Rock Creek, where some small thefts have been reported.

> Very respectfully, your obedient servant,
> R. F. MAURY,
> <u>Colonel First Oregon Cavalry, Commanding</u>.[17]

Following this last work at scouting for the government, Zacheus lived at Roseburg, Oregon where, a couple of years later, the first child of his second family was born. He resided there, in Douglas County, for fourteen years. He then returned to California where he remained for over thirty years, twenty of them at Chico. From there, as the last years of the nineteenth century passed by, the aged Zacheus applied for a pension from the State of Oregon for his services in the Rogue River War of 1855-56. He died in 1910.

And, what happened to Reuben? A granddaughter of Zacheus, Mrs. Edith Farmer Elliot (a professional writer in Portland whose sister was the late movie actress, Frances Farmer), wrote in 1971 that Grandpa Van Ornum refused to keep Reuben "because he was so mean to the little kids, the story has it that Grandpa started back east with him. It is quite possible he ran away back to the Indians and Grandpa let him go . . ."[18]

Zacheus Van Ornum sadly stated in his Oregon pension application in 1902 what he believed to have happened to the captive children:

> My brother was Emigrating to Oregon in 1860 and was MaSSacred by the Indians he lost in money and Property a bout 6000 dollars and 4 of his children taken captive 3 girls one Boy the girls died of Starvation in the goos crek Mountains near Snake Rive the Boy was Rescued by Major McGary in Chash Valley 100 miles north of Salt Lake and I was trying my best to rescue them all the time and government helped me on all and every occasion I spent too years and over $5000 dollars and I think the government would grant me an Indemnity . . ."[19]

APPENDIX I

The Paynes and the Trimbles

Abagel Payne Trimble Utter's family had figured promi-
nently in the westering settlement of her nation's frontier. Her
father, Christopher Columbus Payne, was born in Somerset
County, Pennsylvania in 1786. When he was fourteen his
family moved to the Northwest Territory, to the wilderness that
became Belmont, Ohio. He was a "fearless Indian fighter" and
served as a scout in the War of 1812. Among his exploits was
the defense of Fort Harrison, Indiana Territory with twenty-
four other Indiana Rangers against several hundred beseiging
Indians. At the close of the war he engaged in farming for
three years at Vincennes, Indiana, then to Illinois Territory,
farming nine years in Madison County and three years in San-
gamon County near Springfield. He spent two unsuccessful
years as a miner in the lead region of Galena, either in Illinois
or just across the boundary in Wisconsin. There, his daughter
Abagel was born, 12 July 1827. The Paynes returned to
farming, in Putnam County. In April 1831 Christopher Payne
arrived at Naperville in Du Page County with his wife and
family of six children. They were the second family of settlers
in that county.

The next year the Sauk and Fox Indians made an unsuccessful attempt at keeping one of their villages (where Rock
Island now stands). This was Blackhawk's War and the
Reverend Aaron Payne, a Quaker minister and one of
Christopher's brothers, became its first victim. He was traveling the road from Naperville when he was killed along the Illinois River near Ottawa.[1] "He was captured on his way to his
appointment. He carried no arms, according to the Quaker

custom. The Indians said he was a brave man to travel there in
this way, but even this heroic spirit did not prevent them from
taking his defenseless head and carrying it on a pole."[E] The
Indians took his horse and some money. Although his body
was discovered and buried, his head was never found.

The terrible death of his brother aroused within Christopher
Payne an intense hatred of all Indians. He and his son Uriah
served as volunteers in the Black Hawk war and had several
encounters with the Indians.

George W. Trimble married the eldest Payne daughter in
1832-33. In the latter year Christopher Payne moved his
family to Kane County for two years and became the first
settlers of Batavia, on the Fox River six miles south of
Geneva, Illinois. He then moved on to Squaw Prairie. From
there he made an exploring expedition (that included George
Trimble), which resulted in the discovery of Geneva Lake in
Wisconsin. In early 1836 the Paynes and Trimbles became the
first settlers of Walworth County, Wisconsin. They stayed
only a few months at Geneva Village while a sawmill was
being built. (This Geneva, in Wisconsin, lies fifty miles north
of the residence they once had south of Geneva, Illinois.) The
following January Christopher moved to the outlet of Duck
Lake, later called Lake Como. George Trimble moved to
Walworth. Christopher remained at Duck Lake seven years,
operating his sawmill. Sons, Uriah and George Payne, were
near. In 1844 Christopher Payne moved to the adjoining town
of La Fayette on Sugar Creek.

It was here, on New Year's day 1846, that Abagel (the
youngest Payne daughter) married, bringing another Trimble
into the family. He was born at Mt. Vernon, Ohio twenty-one
years before. A year later Emeline was born to the couple.

Christopher Payne moved soon after to Winnebago
County, purchasing a beautiful farm on the Fox River. A
dispute over ownership of the farm, which he won after two
years of costly court action, led to his sale of the property to
cover his debts. He lived in Fond Du Lac County for a short
time before returning to Walworth County. There, he and his
wife lived upon a portion of the farm of his son-in-law,

George Trimble. Son, George Payne, was living in Columbus County when Christopher went to live with him in 1864. Christopher died in Columbus County seven years later at age eighty-five.

Not all of the relatives stayed in the Illinois-Wisconsin area. Some had gone to Iowa and others on to Oregon. Another of Christopher's brothers (and Abagel's uncles), the Reverend Aaron Payne, had settled in Yamhill County, Oregon Territory. He had been a widower since 1847. All of his family, except one son, had died of consumption.

In addition to the Paynes, there were Trimbles in Oregon by 1860. Abagel's first husband's brother, Pierce H. Trimble, and his family went overland to Linn County in 1853. Another of Abagel's brothers-in-law, Edward Trimble, and his family left Iowa in 1846 and headed for Oregon. Edward also was born at Mt. Vernon, Ohio and was of "Scotch & Irish" descent.[2] The St. Louis *Missouri Republican* on 17 July 1846 reported that some seventeen men had left Oregon on 5 March, coming east and had met Edward Trimble's wagon train.

> The party met the advanced company of the Oregon emigrants at Fort Laramie. They were getting on pretty well, but were suffering from the depredations of the Indians upon their cattle. The Pawnees were principally concerned in these outrages, and on one occasion, attacked and killed one of the emigrants who was out in search of his cattle. The person killed was from Henry county, Iowa, by the name of Edward Trimble. He and a companion by the name of Harrison, were fired upon from the grass, and Trimble killed, and Harrison taken prisoner. They were, however, discovered by two others of the party, who raised the shout, and the Indians fled. Mr. Trimble's body was not found. He has left a wife and four small children. They would have returned with this party, but were prevented from doing so, by peculiar circumstances. Mrs. Trimble's friends may expect her return as speedily as possible.[3]

Edward Trimble was killed by the Pawnees near Scottsbluff. His widow, in her bereavement, was so disheartened by the loss of the cattle that she returned to their home in Iowa with the children. At least two of the children, one son and daughter Martha J. Trimble, later went to Oregon as they were in Salem by 1860. Martha married a wagonmaster and farmer, Joseph M. Pomeroy, in Oregon in 1857. Her husband initially had come across the plains from Illinois to Oregon five years earlier.[4]

APPENDIX II

Wagon Train Taken at City of Rocks, 1860

The Utter and Van Ornum wagon train was the last train to cross the Snake River plains on the Oregon Trail in 1860, but they were not the last to be escorted by the troops stationed on the Portneuf River. Nor were they the only emigrant party to be attacked in the fall of 1860. Simultaneous with the attack on the Utter party, another train was under attack—one hundred and fifty miles to the southeast—at the City of Rocks.

This must have been the last emigrant train to pass Fort Hall that year. It was a small one, half the size of the Utter wagon train with only three or four wagons. In addition to the ox teams there were about one hundred forty head of loose cattle and a few horses. There were a half dozen children from two families. The Herbert Thomas family with Mrs. Thomas' mother, Mrs. Mary Chambers, and Thomas Graham were from La Fayette County, Wisconsin. Richard Eddy was from Wisconsin too. The Josiah Pierce family hailed from Carroll County, Illinois. Five men were also from Illinois, from DeWitt County: the three Brock brothers; John Green; and a German, Henry Ehirenfeld. John Christensen was identified as being from Illinois and California. John Hagerty (or Haggarty) was of Clayton County, Iowa.[1]

Mr. J. C. Wright of Brigham City, Utah Territory, who had reported on the emigrant massacres of the previous year for the *Deseret News*, also acquired an account of this 1860 attack at City of Rocks. His letter and the *Deseret News* interview of John Hagerty form the basis for the following.

This California train arrived at the army encampment of the forces under Lieutenant Colonel Howe by the Portneuf Bridge,

Mrs. Mary Chambers	La Fayette, Co., WI	1
Herbert Thomas		
wife & 4 children	La Fayette, Co., WI	6
Thomas Graham	La Fayette, Co., WI	1
Richard Eddy	WI	1
William Brock	DeWitt Co., IL	1
C. C. Brock	DeWitt Co., IL	1
John W. Brock	DeWitt Co., IL	1
John Green	DeWitt Co., IL	1
Henry Ehirenfeld	DeWitt Co., IL	1
Josiah Pierce		
wife & 2 children	Carroll Co., IL	4
John Christensen	IL & CA	1
John Hagerty (Haggarty)	Clayton Co., IA	1
		20

Members of Wagon Train Attacked at City of Rocks, 1860.

near old Fort Hall, about the 1st of September. Hagerty said the Colonel:

> detailed an escort of ten or twelve men, under Sergeant Barry, to accompany them on their way a few days. After proceeding some sixty or seventy miles, seeing no signs of Indians, the escort returned back on the morning of the 6th, leaving the company to pursue their journey unprotected. Without molestation they proceeded to within five miles of City Rocks, near the junction with the Salt Lake road, where they encamped on the evening of the 7th, by a small stream known as Rapid creek.
>
> At about eleven oclock at night an attack was made on them by a small party of Indians who, on finding the emigrants ready to give them a warm reception, drew off, after firing eight or ten guns, and came up

again on the other side of the camp, where, by taking advantage of the light of the moon which had just risen, they could fire upon the company with greater accuracy, and, at the same time, be hid from the view of the emigrants and measurably secure from their fire.

Wright reported that "the emigrant forces were so feeble that but little hopes of effectual resistance was entertained. However, returning the fire of the enemy, they kept them from making a charge upon the camp that night." John Hagerty stated that the Indians after

continuing the assault about one hour and a half, (during which time they fired some fifty or sixty shots and an indefinite number of arrows, many of which struck the wagons without further injury than perforating them and their contents with holes) they decamped driving off thirty head of cattle, mostly oxen that were used in the teams, which, being tired, had not strayed far from the camp.

As soon as the Indians pulled back that night of the 7th, the emigrants sent for help. Two men, John Brock and Thomas Graham, were dispatched to inform Colonel Howe and his forces on the Portneuf River of the emigrants' predicament and to request assistance.

The emigrants kept up a good watch during the balance of the night, and the next morning picked up twenty-five arrows around their camp, some of which were sticking in their wagons, which had also been pierced with many balls. No Indians were seen, but a sharp look out was kept up during that day and following night, but at about the same time in the evening that the attack was made the night before, thirteen of the oxen that had been driven off returned, which convinced the party that the red skins had not gone far away, and that they were lurking about, seeking for a chance to attack them again under more favorable circumstances than at first.

On the forenoon of the 9th, the emigrants concluded to move their camp about two hundred yards to a more favorable position, but before they had detached all their teams from the wagons, after moving them, the Indians commenced another attack more fierce than the first, as they were in greater force, Mr. Hagerty being of the opinion that they were at least one hundred strong.

Others estimated that the party of Indians firing upon the emigrants to be about sixty in number. In this new position, the defenders could see no chance of saving their lives by solely fighting it out with the attackers, so, they looked for an opportunity to save the women and children. That night the whole party, with the exception of Hagerty, managed to escape by retreating into the bed of the creek among the willows. By retreating up the ravine they were unobserved by the attackers and got away by passing over a mountain. The emigrants took the California Trail back towards Fort Hall where they hoped to reach the soldiers encampment. They had left Hagerty behind,

supposing that he had been killed. He, however, after two or three arrows were shot through his clothes, and several balls had whistled near without striking him, also escaped into the willows, and hid himself, but was watched so closely by the Indians that he could not get away safely, and remained in his hiding place nearly four days, without food, excepting a few berries which he found by crawling about on his hands and knees, to keep out of the sight of the savages, who were watching for him and the rest of the party all the time, evidently supposing that they were yet hid in the brush, and that none of them had made good their escape.

Mr. Hagerty reports that the Indians were at the wagons immediately on their being abandoned by the emigrants, and without waiting to plunder them to any great extent, with much dexterity attached some of the oxen to them and drove off, taking one nearly a mile, the others a less distance, before rifling them of their contents. He is very confident that there were white men among the Indians in disguise.

Others stated that a "medium-sized white man, painted red, with a pair of fine dress boots on, was with the Indians at the attack."[2] John Hagerty

positively saw one individual with short hair, who had on a pair of fine boots, and a pair of pants, but otherwise dressed and painted like an Indian, and when the attacking party were hitching the oxen to the wagons and driving them off, they spoke to the cattle in good English. He says that he was decidedly uneasy during the time he was compelled to remain in the brush, as the Indians were about him in every direction as thick as bees, and he did not know what ultimately might be his fate, neither what had become of those who had got away.

Meanwhile, the two men who had been sent for help (John Brock and Tom Graham) proceeded with all possible speed and overtook the escort under Sergeant Barry before the soldiers even reached their encampment. The soldiers were short of rations, however, and could not go to the relief of the emigrants until the soldiers could be resupplied. When he heard of the attack, Colonel Howe immediately sent out a detachment of twenty-five dragoons under the command of Lieutenant Sanders. They proceeded without delay to the assistance of the emigrant party.

On their march, the troopers intercepted the refugees at Marsh Creek. They "met the women and children almost in a perishing condition, having traveled two days and a half with out food, most of them without shoes, with no more clothing for day or night then they had on when they fled."[3] Their flight through the bushes had torn and ripped off so much of their frail clothing that they scarcely had enough left to be covered. Lieutenant Sanders assisted the emigrants as much as his force could under the circumstances. He left part of his command with the refugees for their protection and proceeded on with the remainder of the dragoons. The rescue force "arrived at the scene of disaster some time on the afternoon of the 12th, much to the joy of Hagerty, who was in a very perilous condition. The Indians on seeing the troops soon hid themselves and kept out of sight." The "stock had all been driven off and the wagons plundered of every article of value they contained." None of the emigrants' property was recovered except for one yoke of oxen. The rest had either been taken away or destroyed, but all of the emigrants had "fortunately escaped without any one being killed or dangerously wounded."[4]

The following morning, the 13th, the troops began their return. According to Mr. Wright, after starting, five or six dragoons who wished to "take an excursion to see if they could not find some of the Indians and gain a little renown by fighting them," obtained permission to do so. They did discover a party of Indians in ambush, and exchanged a few rounds with them. The half-dozen dragoons "got into a bigger fight than they wanted with a few of the rascals who were lying in ambush, upon whom they came unexpectedly, and Hagerty reports that there were some splendid feats of horsemanship performed before they overtook or rejoined the balance of the command." None of the troops were injured.

Lieutenant Sanders gathered the entire party of emigrants and took them back to the encampment on the Portneuf. Colonel Howe did what he could for the dispossessed emigrants, giving the women blankets to use for dresses. From there the emigrants returned with the troops to Camp Floyd. Colonel Howe could recount, "There have traveled West this season over the Port Neuf River Bridge, by register kept 769 men, 325 women, 474 children with 359 wagons, 1045 horses, 4075 cattle, 3415 sheep, and East 16 men and 200 horses."[5]

Mr. J. C. Wright received his information about the City of Rocks attack, and wrote from Brigham City, Utah Territory, on 27 September 1860:

Report reached this place last night of another Indian outrage upon a small party of emigrants from Illinois on their way to California, by Landers Wagon Route.

This statement was made by a gentleman who received it from one of the party, and I presume, as far as it goes, may be relied upon as being substantially correct.

Mr. Wright's letter was published in the Salt Lake City *Deseret News* on 3 October 1860, as was the following two articles:

Return of the Troops from Fort Hall.

Yesterday morning, between 9 and 10 oclock, companies E and H of the second Dragoons, under the command of Lieut. Norris, passed through the city *en route* for Camp Floyd. They numbered 86 men and 4 officers, with 18 mule wagons. They left Portneuf on the 24th of Sept., and will reach Camp tomorrow. Accompanying them are about 20 men, women, children, of the emigrant company alluded to elsewhere in this issue.[6]

INDIAN HOSTILITIES ON THE NORTHERN ROUTE.

After the communication of Hon. J. C. Wright, published in this number, was in type, Mr. John Hagerty, one of the emigrants who was in the company attacked and despoiled by the Indians, near City of Rocks, to which occurrence the communication refers, called at our office and gave a full detail of the assault and robbery . . .

How many more small straggling companies of
emigrants, passing over that route late in the season,
will be used up before it becomes generally known
that they cannot travel safely in that manner, is not
known. In this instance, it was fortunate indeed that
all the persons escaped unhurt.

The *Sacramento Union* on 31 October told about one small
wagon trains experience with the Indians:

OVERLAND TRAIN.—A train of six wagons, drawn
by three and four ox teams each, and fifty-four head of
loose stock, passed down I street, yesterday, on its
way to Cache creek. The party, consisting of several
families and a liberal supply of children, left Lincoln
county, Missouri, on the 24th day of April last, and
have been on their long and tedious journey since.
Along the route they have met many parties of Indians,
who were found generally friendly and in no way disposed to interrupt or molest them in their journey. But
the parties informed us that at various points, and under the most unfavorable circumstances, they were
molested by "White Indians," who seemed determined
to drive off their stock. It was by the utmost exertions
and vigilant watchings, that their stock was saved
from these white rascals.[7]

When the *Deseret News* printed the accounts and accompanying remarks of the attack of the train at City of Rocks, the
news of the disaster that befell the Utter wagon train had not
yet reached Salt Lake City. When news of the rescue of the
Utter survivors did reach Utah Territory, on 12 December the
Deseret News reported:[8]

Captain Dent's report was exciting much indignation
against the Indians, who made the attack, and great
military operations, for the protection of emigrants
from the States to Oregon next summer, were proposed . . .

APPENDIX III

Roberts Visits Utter Massacre Sites

A. B. Roberts of Walla Walla had heard the whole story of the Utter massacre from Mrs. Chase in late 1860. The summer of 1861, his sister and brother and their families were journeying over the Oregon Trail to join him. Roberts wished to aid his siblings and gathered seven packs of provisions and five or six saddle horses for the trip into the Snake country. He hired James Veasey to help with the pack string. Angus McKay offered to go too. Since a Mr. T. P. Denny had a son and family also emigrating to Walla Walla, Mr. Denny sent another son, Than, and a hired man, Henry Calkins, to accompany Roberts. The party of five stopped by the Umatilla Indian Agency where Agent George Abbott warned them of the dangers of the trip, "You won't last 24 hours after you reach Grand Ronde." At the agency, the group were joined by Henry Watson and his father who also were going along the Trail to meet friends.[1]

The Roberts party started soon after Independence Day and tarried in the Grand Ronde and Powder River valleys to do some prospecting for gold. They met a group of wary Umatilla Indians; "these two Valleys were disputed ground between the Umatillas and the Shoshone tribes and either party coming into Powder River or Grand Ronde Valley was expected to be on the fight."

As the party entered the Snake country, they adopted more cautious tactics for traveling and camping. They struck the Snake at Farewell Bend and dug a "rifle pit on the level plain near the river where we could see the approach of an enemy more than a gun shot away and if necessary we could take shelter behind the nearby river banks." Roberts figured that with the deep rifle pits they "were always safe, and while the Indians often had signal fires in many directions around us, they dared not make an attack" on the camp, and "during our traveling hours we feared no one." While at Farewell Bend they visited the site of the Van Ornum massacre and found "many interesting papers and a lock of golden hair evidently torn from some poor woman's head as she made her deathly struggle against the savage fiend."

> The next day 22 miles brought us to the Malheur where we stopped at noon and spent the balance of the day—spending much time in bathing in a fine pool and giving our horses also a great bath, taking them in separately and learning them and ourselves to swim together.
>
> During the afternoon Henry Watson and I went upon the great butte [Malheur Butte] across the river where we could see for many miles around. We could see a great camp of nearly 1,000 Indian wigwams down towards Snake river but no emigrants on the road to the East.

Roberts and his group traveled on to the Owyhee and followed the South Alternate. They visited the site of the Utter massacre and viewed "burned wagons, bones of dead horses, remnants of books and valuable papers, locks of human hair and the evidence of the very shallow burial of the dead, which was done by a company of cavalry."

The party of seven attempting to meet the emigrants, went on to the Bruneau and some on to Three Island Crossing. Finding no evidence of the emigration they retraced their path to the west. When they reached their planned camping place at the Owyhee crossing, they

> met a "big scare" again. Below us and near the Snake and Owyhee were what looked to be 1000 Indian wigwams. The Watsons refused to go into camp and

proposed to push on 20 miles more to the Malheur in the night. I said no to this and proceeded to select a sure location and to unpack the tired animals. At near sundown the Watsons and Dennys pulled out for the Malheur.

We dug our rifle pit near the river on the edge of the smooth level plain; nearby us was a little bunch of willows, from our position we could see our enemy approaching for over a quarter of a mile.

By ten o'clock the Indians had "signal fires" all about us. Soon after 12 I called to McKay and called his attention to the Indian fires; he very cooly said: "Well, let them come." But they didn't come and at sunrise Veasey had a good breakfast ready and we packed up and started on our way over the plains to the Malheur expecting that we would meet Indians coming back from an attack and probable murder of the Watson-Denny party; but we had little fear of an attack upon us in daylight.

Well, we arrived safely and to our dismay we found that my "cache" of three pack loads of provisions had been dug up and was gone. Later I learned that the Watson party had met Capt. A. D. Pierce with a party of prospectors who was getting short and told him that they had a cache which they could not need and that he was welcome to the supplies.

So we pushed on and saw no human being until we reached the Umatilla.

The relatives and friends of A. B. Roberts did cross the Snake Country safely; they were with Captain Crawford's escort for several hundred miles. The first weary wagon train that exited the Snake Country "reported almost continuous conflict with Indians after crossing the Rockies and all the way down the Snake river." The train led by Samuel King fought with the Indians at the Owyhee. (Roberts noted that some of the 1861 emigrants actually located homes, the first, in the Grande Ronde valley.)

APPENDIX IV

1861 Attack on the Harriman Train

On 8 August 1861 the Harriman train was attacked on the California Trail in the City of Rocks area (just northeast of where the borders of Idaho, Utah, and Nevada adjoin). The following versions disagree only on the number of horses lost and the time of day that events occurred. According to an account reprinted in the *Sacramento Union* on 9 September 1861, the

train embraced seventy-five people, forty of whom were men, the balance women and children. They had eleven wagons and fourteen horses and eighty-eight head of horned cattle. Their trip was a prosperous and happy one, until they reached the City of Rocks. Early one morning, when about to resume their journey, they were surrounded by forty persons disguised as Indians, but who were, as it was subsequently disclosed by their distinct language, whites, and some of the party were recognized as Mormons.

The emigrants were told by these marauders that nothing was desired of them but their stock, and give it up they must. The terrified emigrants immediately commenced preparing themselves for defense, and under instructions of a pious disciple, some of them were praying for the assistance of Providence, when the unchristian-like rascals stampeded their stock, and that was the last seen of it, leaving on the ground the horseless wagons and their unhappy owners.

The party, minus their stock, after a short time, concluded to proceed upon their journey, and packed upon the back of those who were able all the necessaries of life their wagons contained, leaving them empty. No lives were lost on either side, and we have not learned that a single shot was fired by either party. In this condition they traveled to Humboldt City, from 300 to 400 miles, arriving in a nearly destitute condition on Monday last, the 2d inst. The females and children had barely sufficient clothing to cover their persons, and were in many instances barefooted, or nearly so. The atmosphere at this season is unpleasantly cold at night, and their sufferings from the insufficiency of clothing and food must have been great, not to say torturing. On their way to Humboldt City they were overtaken by another train of three wagons, under Capt. Brown. We learn that he did everything in his power to alleviate their sufferings, giving his third wagon to the exhausted, enabling them to recruit. He also gave them a third of his remaining provisions. Still nearer, they came upon the trains of Capts. Winters and Childs, who divided their provisions with the unfortunate members of the train, and assisted them in every possible manner. At Humboldt City the citizens treated them kindly, and authorized Waters, Whitney and Rutherford to come west and inform the residents of Nevada of the circumstances of the case, and appeal to the citizens for much required aid.[1]

The recently opened army post of Fort Churchill was located just east of the mining community of Carson City in the newly created mining territory of Nevada. A unit of the 1st Dragoons garrisoned the post. In early September, Second Lieutenant E. M. Baker

proceeded with a detachment, consisting of one noncommissioned officer and ten men, and a wagon containing provisions, for the purpose of assisting such emigrants as were absolutely in need of it. I found about thirty miles from this post (on the Carson River) a party of emigrants, about fifty in number, who had been attacked and robbed of everything (except what they had on their backs) about sixty-five miles northeast [northwest] of Salt Lake. They stated that the party who attacked them were Indians, commanded by white men. They were attacked on the night of the 8th of August, and lost all their animals on the night of the 9th. They have since walked the whole distance to the Carson River, receiving such assistance from other trains as they were able to give them. I distributed 400 pounds of flour, 300 pounds of pork, 26 pounds of rice, 44 pounds of sugar, 60 pounds coffee, and 1 quart of salt, which, with the assistance received from the citizens of Virginia and Carson Cities, will be sufficient to last them until they reach their destination. The women and children belonging to the party were brought to this post, and have since gone on to Carson and Virginia.[2]

In transmitting Baker's report to Department of Pacific Headquarters on 10 September, the commander of the post, Lieutenant Colonel George A. H. Blake, stated that the party of emigrants

were robbed by the Indians this side of Salt Lake. According to the statement of Mr. S. M. Harriman, in charge of the train, to me, the train consisted of 74 persons, 11 wagons, 89 head of work cattle, 5 horses, and 2 mules, which was the total number of the party when attacked. The total number brought into this post was 54, viz, 22 men, 13 women, and 19 children. The train was attacked on the night of the 8th of August, and abandoned on the morning of the 9th of August, 1861. Almost daily emigrant trains are passing in want of provisions, and I have issued such quantities necessary to carry them to the settlements, and for which I would ask the approval of the general commanding the department.

Notes

Abbreviations used in Text

The major sources of information for the *Utter Disaster* are mainly cited in the text by a letter in superscript, instead of being referenced with an Arabic numeral:

D   Frederick T. Dent, Report of 8 November 1860, Fort Walla Walla, 36th Congress, 2nd Session, House, *Ex. Doc. No 29*, 86-90.

E   Emeline L. Trimble Fuller, *Left by the Indians* (Mt. Vernon, IA: Hawk-eye Steam Print, 1892). (Also reissued, New York: Edward Eberstadt, 1936; rpt. Malheur Country Review, Vol. V, No. 4-9 (March - August 1984).)

M   Joseph Myers, from the following four sources:

1. ———, "The Late Salmon Falls Massacre," *Portland Christian Advocate*, 15 November 1860, rpt. *Olympia* (W.T.) *Pioneer and Democrat*, 23 November 1860, also rpt. *Olympia* (W.T.) *Washington Standard*, 30 November 1860.

2. ———, "Adventures of the Rescued Immigrants," *Salem Oregon Statesman*, 26 November 1860; rpt. *Sacramento Union*, 4 December 1860.

3. ———, "The Snake River Massacre—Account by one of the Survivors," *Oregon City Argus*, 24 November 1860.

4. ———, *Portland Advertiser*, 12 November 1860; rpt. as "The Surviving Emigrants," *Port Townsend* (W. T.) *North-West*, 29 November 1860; also rpt. in *Portland Oregonian*, 17 November 1860.

IM   Isabella Myers Martin, in Fred Lockley's column, "Impressions and Observations of the Journal Man," *Oregon Journal* (Portland), 1 & 2 December 1922.

MM   Margaret Myers Beers, Private manuscript, Salem, OR, 11 April 1927.

Abbreviations used in Notes

AGO   US   Department of War. *Letters Received by the Office of the Adjutant General (Main Series), 1822-60.*

CIA   Commissioner of Indian Affairs.

NARS Washington DC: National Archives and Records Service, General Services Administration.

OIA   US Bureau of Indian Affairs. *Letters Received by the Office of Indian Affairs 1824-81, M234: Oregon Superintendency, 1842-1880.* NARS.

OSIA   *Records of the Oregon Superintendency of Indian Affairs, 1848-73, M2: Vol. G, September 1859-July 1861.* NARS.

SIA   Superintendent of Indian Affairs.

WR   *War of the Rebellion*, Series I, Vol. L, Parts I & II.

WSIA *Records of the Washington Superintendency of Indian Affairs, 1853-74, M5.* NARS.

Chapter 1

1. Myers, "The Late Salmon Falls Massacre;" Myers, "The Snake River Massacre—Account by one of the Survivors;" Emeline L. Trimble Fuller. See explanation under Notes.

2. Foregoing from Emeline.

3. Marriage Record 236, Walworth County Register of Deeds, Elkhorn, WI.

4. Margaret Myers Beers. See explanation under Notes.

5. Myers; Emeline; Margaret Myers; Isabella Myers; Captain Frederick T. Dent (see explanation under Notes); *1855 Wisconsin State Census*; *Tenth Census, 1880: Oregon Soundex M620*; *Twelfth Census, 1900: Oregon Soundex M620*; *Twelfth Census, 1900: Oregon, Morrow Co., 9 Dry Fork Pct.*; "The Unfortunate Immigrants," *Sacramento Union*, 22 November 1860.

6. Merrill J. Mattes, *The Great Platte River Road*, 8-9.

7. Mattes, 40.

8. Aubrey L. Haines, *Historic Sites Along the Oregon Trail*.

9. Myers; John C. W. Bailey, *Kane County (IL) Directory for 1859-60*; Dr Robert F. Barnes, Letter to Author, Batavia, IL, 7 December 1990.

10. *1855 Wisconsin Census*. Also Pioneer File Index, Portland: Oregon Historical Society.

11. Zacheus Van Ornum [Zachias Van Orman], Pension Application #1269, Oregon Historical Society. (There were 17 items in two files, both #1269, prior to 12 November 1991 when they were consolidated into one.)

12. *Seventh Census, 1850: Wisconsin, Lafayette Co., 353, Wiota Town*; *Ninth Census, 1870: Oregon, Douglas Co., 4, Coles Valley Pct.*; *Tenth Census, 1880: Oregon Soundex U360 [nine], V565*; George H. Abbott, "The Massacre of 1860," *Idaho Historical Society Reports*, Vol. 1, No. 3 (1 October 1908), 25-32; *OIA*, Roll 612: Edward R. Geary to CIA, 7 November 1860, 457-60 and George H. Abbott to SIA, 30 October 1860, 461-65; "Another Indian Massacre," *Port Townsend North-West*, 25 October 1860; and Newell Hart, *The Bear River Massacre*, 62.

13. Myers; Emeline; *Tenth Census, 1880: Oregon Soundex R300*; Isabella Myers; "Jacob Rieth," *History of the Pacific Northwest: Oregon and Washington*, Vol II, 534-35.

14. Miles Cannon, "Sinker Creek Tragedy of Early Pioneer Days," *Boise Idaho Statesman*, 17, 24, 31 July, 7, 14, 21 August 1921 also Idaho Historical Society, Ms 70 Fed. Writers Project, Bx #2, n. d.; "The News," *Portland Oregonian*, 6 October 1860; Isabella Myers.

Chapter 2

1.   Department of War, *Returns From Regular Army Cavalry Regiments, 1833-1916, M744*, Roll 17; "The Surviving Emigrants," *Port Townsend North-West*, 29 November 1860. See explanation under notes.

2.   Report of Major Enoch Steen, 18 August 1860, *AGO, M567*, Roll 629, No. 9; Dixons report on Steens expedition in "Report of the Secretary of War," Senate, *Ex. Doc. No. 64*, App. IX, 537.

3.   C. B. Wiley, "Pioneer of 1860, Tillamook, Oregon," *Oregon Journal,* 5 March 1927, reprinted in Fred Lockley, *Conversations with Bullwhackers . . . .*

4.   Report of Major Steen, 23 August 1860, *AGO, M567*, Roll 629, No. 9.

5.   Emeline; Myers; Isabella Myers.

6.   *AGO M567*, Roll 634; *Returns From Cavalry Regiments, M744*, Roll 17 and *M617*, Roll 595.

7.   Cannon, "Sinker Creek Tragedy of Early Pioneer Days."

8.   *Returns From Cavalry Regiments, M744*, Roll 17; *Register of Enlistments in the United States Army, 1798-1914, M233*, Roll 25.

9.   Myers; Abbott to SIA, 30 October 1860; "Attack Upon an Emigrant Train," *Olympia Pioneer and Democrat*, 12 October 1860.

10.   *Returns From Cavalry Regiments, M744*, Roll 17; *Register of Enlistments , M233*, Roll 26; Emeline.

11.   Myers; Margaret Myers.

12.   William H. Hector, SIA, to B/Gen Benjamin Alvord, Salem, Oregon, 11 July 1862, *WR*, II, 16-17.

13.   Myers; Abbott to SIA, 30 October 1860; Margaret Myers.

14.   Haines.

15.   Emeline; Cannon, "Sinker Creek Tragedy of Early Pioneer Days."

Chapter 3

1 Cannon, "A Train on the Oregon Trail and Its Last Camp In the Desert," *Boise Capital News*, 5 December 1915, sec. 2. This action by the ex-dragoons was not included in Cannon's subsequent accounts.

2. Cannon, "A Train on the Oregon Trail . . ." The foregoing from Myers; Emeline; Margaret Myers; Cannon, "A Train on the Oregon Trail . . ." and "Sinker Creek Tragedy of Early Pioneer Days;" Abbott, "The Massacre of 1860;" "The News," *Portland Oregonian*, 6 October 1860.

3. A. B. Roberts, "Fragments of Early History," *Up To The Times*, March-April 1911, 3346.

4. Foregoing from Myers; Emeline; Margaret Myers; Cannon; Abbott, "The Massacre of 1860;" Roberts, 3346-47.

5. Cannon, "A Train on the Oregon Trail . . ." and "Sinker Creek Tragedy of Early Pioneer Days."

6. Foregoing from Myers; Emeline; Margaret Myers; Cannon; Abbott, "The Massacre of 1860;" Abbott to SIA, 30 October 1860.

7. Following from Myers; Emeline; Margaret Myers; Isabella Myers; Abbott, "The Massacre of 1860;" Roberts; George E. Cole, "Willow Creek O., Oct 1, 1860," *Port Townsend North-West*, 11 October 1860.

8. Following from Myers; Emeline; Margaret Myers; Abbott, "The Massacre of 1860;" Cannon; Abbott to SIA, 30 October 1860.

9. Cannon, "A Train on the Oregon Trail . . ."

10. Abbott, "The Massacre of 1860."

11. Abbott, "The Massacre of 1860;" Abbott to SIA, 30 October 1860.

12. Foregoing from Myers; Emeline; Cannon.

Chapter 4

1. Foregoing from Myers; Emeline; Margaret Myers; Cannon; Abbott to SIA, 30 October 1860.

2. Foregoing from Myers; Emeline; Margaret Myers.

3. Foregoing from Myers; Emeline; Margaret Myers.

4. Abbott, "The Massacre of 1860;" Abbott to SIA, 30 October 1860.

5. Dixon's report on Steen's expedition, 528-41; Gen. Harney's letter, 25 April 1860 & Wallen's Map, *AGO, M567*, Roll 629; Gregory M. Franzwa, *Oregon Trail Revisited*; Chris Moore, "The Terrible Trail: Nelson Works To See Meek Cut-off Marked," *Ontario* (OR) *Argus Observer*, 6 February 1976, Supplement.

6. Abbott, "The Massacre of 1860."

7. Following from Abbott, "The Massacre of 1860;" Abbott to SIA, 30 October 1860; Emeline; Myers.

Chapter 5

1. The information for this chapter is entirely from Myers; Emeline; Margaret Myers; except for the two quotes from Cannon.

2. Cannon.

3. Leo F. Young, conversation at Author's home, 24 May 1990, Caldwell, ID.

4. Cannon.

Chapter 6

1. Myers; Abbott to SIA, 30 October 1860; "Attack Upon an Emigrant Train," *Olympia Pioneer and Democrat*, 12 October 1860.

2. Pioneer File Index, Portland: Oregon Historical Society.

3. Abbott, "The Massacre of 1860."

4. Myers; Abbott, "The Massacre of 1860;" Cole; Abbott to SIA, 30 October 1860; *Olympia Pioneer and Democrat*, 12 October 1860.

5. "Shocking Murder of Forty-five Emigrants by the Snake Indians," *Port Townsend North-West*, 11 October 1860; Coles letter follows.

6. "The News," *Portland Oregonian*, 6 October 1860; "The Salmon River Massacre," *Sacramento Union*, 11 October 1860; and "Important From the Pacific," *New York Times*, 23 October 1860; followed by "Forty-five Emigrants murdered by Indians," *Sacramento Bee*, 9 October 1860.

7. *Olympia Pioneer and Democrat*, 12 October 1860.

8. *OSIA*, Roll 8, 174-5.

9. Edward R. Geary to CIA, 4 October 1860, *OIA*, Roll 612.

10. "The Massacre," *Olympia Pioneer and Democrat*, 19 October 1860.

11. Abbott, "The Massacre of 1860;" Myers; Pioneer File Index, Portland: Oregon Historical Society.

12. Abbott, "The Massacre of 1860."

13. Abbott, "The Massacre of 1860;" Abbott to SIA, 30 October 1860; Byron N. Dawes, Letter to Army, 3 October 1860, Umatilla Reservation, *AGO, M567*, Roll 629.

14. "Another Indian Massacre," *Port Townsend North-West*, 25 October 1860; "Oregon," *New York Times*, 5 November 1860.

15. Abbott, "The Massacre of 1860;" and the foregoing, also Abbott to SIA, 30 October 1860.

16. Geary to Abbott, 10 October 1860, *OSIA*, Roll 8.

Chapter 7

1. Abbott, "The Massacre of 1860."

2. Col. George Wright, Report of 10 October 1860, Fort Vancouver, W. T., *AGO, M567*, Roll 629, No. 11.

3. Wright, Military Letter to Governor of Oregon, 18 October 1860, Portland: Oregon State Historical Society, Mss 1514, Military, Misc. File.

4. "News From Washington," *New York Times*, 15 November 1860.

5. "Army Intelligence," *Olympia Pioneer and Democrat*, 2 November 1860.

6. Department of War, *Returns From United States Military Posts, 1800-1916, M617*, Roll 285.

7. *Returns From Military Posts, M617*, Roll 285; *Eighth Census, 1860: Washington T., Walla Walla Co., 303-310 Garrison Ft. Walla Walla;* George W. Cullum, *Biographical Register of the Officers and Graduates of the US Military Academy, 1802-1890*, 3rd Ed., vol. 1 and 2.

8. Abbott to SIA, 30 October 1860.

9. Abbott, "The Massacre of 1860."

10. Cornelius J. Brosnan, *History of Idaho*, 111; Lalia Boone, *Idaho Place Names*.

Chapter 8

1. "Twelve of the Lost Train Found Alive!" *Oregon City Argus*, 10 November 1860.

2. Myers; Dent; Abbott, "The Massacre of 1860;" *Seventh Census: Wisconsin, Lafayette Co., 353, Wiota Town*.

3. Abbott, "The Massacre of 1860;" "P. D. Wood Finds traces of Oregon Trail," *200 Years In The Making*.

4. Cannon, "A Train on the Oregon Trail . . ."

5. Margaret Myers; Isabella Myers.

6. Myers; Dent; Abbott, "The Massacre of 1860;" *Seventh Census: Wisconsin, Lafayette Co., 353, Wiota Town*.

7. Emeline; Margaret Myers.

8. Dent, "Homeward Bound," Report of 28 October 1860, Camp on Burnt River, *AGO, M567*, Roll 629.

9. Emeline; Dent; *Returns From Cavalry Regiments, M744*, Roll 5.

Chapter 9

1. Abbott to SIA, 30 October 1860; Capt. A. J. Smith to G. H. Abbott, 31 October 1860, *OIA*, Roll 612, 456.

2. O. C. Harcum, Letter "Walla Walla, Nov. 1st, 1860," *Portland Advertiser*, 6 November 1860; rpt. *Oregon City Argus*, 10 November 1860; rpt. *Olympia Pioneer and Democrat*, 16 November 1860.

3. "Twelve of the Lost Train Found Alive!" *Oregon City Argus*, 10 November 1860.

4. "The Suffering Immigrants North," *Sacramento Union*, 15 November 1860.

5. Abbott, "The Massacre of 1860."

6. Geary to CIA, 7 November 1860, *OIA*.

7. Col. George Wright, Report of 7 November 1860, Fort Vancouver, W. T., *AGO, M567*, Roll 629, No. 12.

8. Margaret Myers; and "The Suffering Emigrants," *Portland Oregonian*, 17 November 1860.

9. Roberts, 3347.

10. Roberts, 3289.

11. "The Suffering Emigrants," *Portland Oregonian*, 17 November 1860.

12. "The Unfortunate Immigrants," *Sacramento Union*, 22 November 1860.

13. Myers; "The Suffering Emigrants," *Portland Oregonian*, 17 November 1860; Zacheus Van Ornum, Pension Application.

14. "The Suffering Emigrants," *Portland Oregonian*, 17 November 1860; Isabella Myers; *Tenth Census, 1880: Oregon Soundex M620*.

15. Isabella Myers; Cannon, "Sinker Creek Tragedy of Early Pioneer Days."

16. "Summary of News," *Portland Oregonian*, 22 December 1860.

17. Myers; *Returns From Cavalry Regiments, M744*, Roll 17; *Register of Enlistments, M233*, Roll 26.

18. A. D. Moses, "Pioneer Resident Reviews History of Local Emigrants Indian Massacre Near Site of Former Owyhee Ford," *Gate City J.*, 16 October 1958.

19. Lewis A. McArthur, *Oregon Geographic Names*; "Louis Rieth," *Portland Oregonian*, 23 September 1926. Following is from "Jacob Rieth," *History of the Pacific*

Northwest; Ninth Census, 1870: Oregon, Umatilla Co., Pendleton to Willow Creek Pct.

20. "Jacob Rieth," *History of the Pacific Northwest.*

21. *Tenth Census, 1880: Oregon, Umatilla Co., 19 Pendleton Pct.*; A. D. Moses.

Chapter 10

1. Zacheus Van Ornum.
2. Metat Kues, *Portland Times*, 19 December 1860, Vol. I, No. 1.
3. "The Captives," *Portland Times*, 19 December 1860.
4. "Summary of News," *Portland Oregonian*, 22 December 1860.
5. Colonel George Wright, Letter to Governor of Oregon, Fort Vancouver, 3 January 1861, *WR*, I, 430.
6. A. J. Cain to Edward R. Geary, SIA, 1 May 1861, *WSIA*, Roll 21, 196.
7. Cain to Geary, 9 July 1861, *WSIA*, Roll 21, 198-99.
8. Mattes, 540, from diary of Charles A. Scott.
9. Cain to Geary, 9 July 1861.
10. Boone.

Chapter 11

1. B/Gen Benjamin Alvord, Letter to Oregon SIA, Fort Vancouver, 8 July 1862, *WR*, II, 10.
2. OSIA to Alvord, 11 July 1862.
3. Lt. William B. Hughes to Lt. Col. Reuben F. Maury, Fort Vancouver, 12 July 1862, *WR*, II, 20.
4. James H. Martineau, "Military History of Cache Valley," *Tullidge's Quarterly Magazine*, vol. 2 (April 1882) #1: 125.
5. Col. Justus Steinberger to Lt. Col. Reuben F. Maury, Fort Walla Walla,11 August 1862, *WR*, II, 61-62.
6. Steinberger.

7.   "August 19-October 11, 1862.—Expedition against the Snake Indians in Idaho," *WR*, I, 166-69.

8.   Col. P. Edward Connor to Maj. Edward McGarry, Camp Douglas, 20 November 1862, *WR*, II, 228-29.

9.   Dale L. Morgan, ed., "Washaskie and the Shoshoni, Part VII—1862-1863," *Annals of Wyoming* 28, no. 2 (October 1956): 193.

10.   Hart, 62.

11.   Praben A. Hansen, "More About the Battle Creek," *Preston* (ID) *Franklin County Citizen,* 21 February 1918.

12.   "Expedition for the Recovery of a Captive," *Salt Lake City* (UT) *Deseret News*, 26 November 1862.

13.   "November 20-27, 1862.—Expedition from Camp Douglas to the Cache Valley, Utah Ter.," *WR*, I, 181-83.

14.   Henry C. Haskin, "Letter from Camp Douglas, U. T.," *Napa County* (CA) *Reporter*, 20 December 1862.

15.   Zacheus Van Ornum, Pension Application; Hart, 58.

16.   Zacheus Van Ornum, Pension Application.

17.   "August 27-October 5, 1864.—Expedition from Fort Boise to Salmon Falls, Idaho Ter.," *WR*, I, 386-90.

18.   Hart, 61-62.

19.   Zacheus Van Ornum, Pension Application.

Appendix I

1.   Foregoing from John A. Gustafson, *Historic Batavia; History of Walworth County, Wisconsin*; and Emeline.

2.   Pioneer File Index, Portland: Oregon Historical Society. The foregoing from Emeline; and Gustafson.

3.   Dale L. Morgan, *Overland in 1846*, Vol. II, 602.

4.   Miles Cannon, *Toward the Setting Sun*, 133; Emeline; Pioneer File Index, Portland: Oregon Historical Society.

Appendix II

1.   J. C. Wright, "Another Indian Outrage," *Deseret News*, 3 October 1860 and "Indian Hostilities On the Northern

Route," same issue. These two accounts, the second from John Hagerty, form the basis for the following discription of attack at City of Rocks in 1860. Also *AGO, M567*, Roll 634 for listing of emigrants.

2. J. C. Wright.
3. J. C. Wright.
4. Preceding and following: Wright; Hagerty.
5. *AGO, M567*, Roll 634.
6. "Return of the Troops from Fort Hall," *Deseret News*, 3 October 1860.
7. "Overland Train," *Sacramento Union*, 31 October 1860.
8. "Western News By Mail," *Deseret News*, 12 December 1860.

Appendix III

1. This and following from Roberts, 3291-92 and 3345-3349.

Appendix IV

1. "The Robbery of the Immigration," *Sacramento Union*, 9 September 1861.
2. "August 8-9, 1861.—Attack on Emigrant Train near the Great Salt Lake, Utah Ter.," *WR*, I, 24.

Bibliography

Bailey, John C. W. *Kane County (IL) Directory for 1859-60*. Chicago: Press and Tribune Steam Book and Job Print, 1859.

Beers, Margaret Myers. Private manuscript, Salem, OR, 11 April 1927.

Boise Capital News, 5 December 1915.

Boise Idaho Statesman. July-August 1921.

Boone, Lalia. *Idaho Place Names*. Moscow, ID: University of Idaho Press, 1988.

Brosnan, Cornelius J. *History of Idaho*. New York: Scribners, 1918.

Cannon, Miles. *Toward the Setting Sun*. Portland, OR: Columbian Press, 1953.

Cullum, George W. *Biographical Register of the Officers and Graduates of the U.S. Military Academy, 1802-1890*. 3rd Ed. 2 vols. Boston: Houghton, Mifflin & Co., 1891.

Franzwa, Gregory M. *The Oregon Trail Revisited*, 3rd ed. Gerald, MO: Patrice Press, May 1983.

Fuller, Emeline L. Trimble. *Left by the Indians*. Mt. Vernon, IA: Hawk-eye Steam Print, 1892. (Also reissued, New York: Edward Eberstadt, 1936.)

Gate City J. 16 October 1958.

Gustafson, John A. *Historic Batavia*. Batavia, IL: Batavia Historical Society.

Hailey, John. *The History of Idaho*. Boise: Syms-York Co, 1910.

Haines, Aubrey L. *Historic Sites Along the Oregon Trail*. Gerald, MO: Patrice Press, 1981.

Hart, Newell. *The Bear River Massacre*. Preston, ID: Cache Valley Newsletter Publishing, 1982.

History of the Pacific Northwest: Oregon and Washington. Vol. II. Portland, OR: North Pacific History, 1889.

History of Walworth County, Wisconsin. Chicago: Western Historical Company, 1882.

Idaho Historical Society Reports, vol. 1, no. 3 (1 October 1908).

Jones, Larry. "Otter Massacre Site." *Reference Series 233.* Boise: Idaho Historical Society, March 1982.

Lockley, Fred. *Conversations with Bullwhackers, Muleskinners, Pioneers, Prospectors, '49ers, Indian Fighters, Trappers, Ex-Barkeepers, Authors, Preachers, Poets & Near Poets & All Sorts & Conditions of Men.* Comp. and ed. Mike Helm. Eugene, OR: Rainy Day Press, 1981.

Madsen, Brigham D. *Shoshoni Frontier and the Bear River Massacre.* Salt Lake City: University of Utah Press, 1985.

Martin, Isabella Myers. In Fred Lockley's column, "Impressions and Observations of the Journal Man." *Oregon Journal* (Portland), 1 & 2 December 1922.

Mattes, Merrill J. *The Great Platte River Road.* Lincoln: University of Nebraska Press, 1969.

McArthur, Lewis A. *Oregon Geographic Names.* 5th ed. Portland: Western Imprints: The Press of the Oregon Historical Society, 1982.

Morgan, Dale L. *Overland in 1846: Diaries & Letters of the California-Oregon Trail.* Georgetown, CA: Talisman Press, 1963, Vol. II.

———. Ed. "Washaskie and the Shoshoni, Part VI—1862." *Annals of Wyoming* 28, no. 1 (April 1956).

Napa County (CA) Reporter. December 20, 1862.

New York Times. October-November 1860.

Olympia (W.T.) Pioneer and Democrat. October-November 1860.

Olympia Washington Standard. 30 November 1860.

Ontario (OR) Argus Observer. 6 February 1976.

Oregon City (OR) Argus. November 1860.

Oregon State Historical Society, Portland. Mss 1514, Military, Misc. File.

————. Pension Application #1269.

————. Pioneer File Index.

Port Townsend (W. T.) *North-West.* October-November 1860.

Portland Oregonian. October-December 1860; September 1926.

Portland (OR) *Times.* 19 December 1860.

Preston (ID) *Franklin County Citizen.* 21 February 1918.

Sacramento Bee. 9 October 1860.

Sacramento Union. September-December 1860.

Salem Oregon Statesman. 26 November 1860.

Salt Lake City Deseret News. October 1860-November 1862.

Tullidge's Quarterly Magazine (Salt Lake City: Star Printing), vol. 2 (April 1882) #1.

Unruh, John D., Jr. *The Plains Across.* Urbana: University of Illinois Press, 1979.

Up To The Times (Walla Walla Publishing), March-April 1911.

US Bureau of the Census. *Seventh Census of the United States, 1850.*

————. *Eighth Census of the United States, 1860.*

————. *Ninth Census of the United States, 1870.*

————. *Tenth Census of the United States, 1880.*

————. *Twelfth Census of the United States, 1900.*

US Bureau of Indian Affairs. *Letters Received by the Office of Indian Affairs 1824-81, M234: Oregon Superintendency, 1842-1880.* Washington DC: National Archives and Records Service, General Services Administration (NARS), 1958, Roll 612.

————. *Records of the Oregon Superintendency of Indian Affairs, 1848-73, M2: Vol. G, September 1859-July 1861.* NARS, 1940, Roll 8.

————. *Records of the Washington Superintendency of Indian Affairs, 1853-74, M5.* NARS, Roll 21.

US Congress.

————. 36th Congress, 2nd Session. House, *Ex. Doc. No. 29,* 86-90.

————. 37th Congress, 2nd Session, 1861-62. "Report of the Secretary of War." Vol. 2, Senate, *Ex. Doc. No. 64*, App. IX. Serial 1118.

————. 37th Congress, 3rd Session, 1861-62. Senate, *Ex. Doc. No. 17.* Serial 1149.

US Department of War. *Letters Received by the Office of the Adjutant General (Main Series), 1822-60, M567.* NARS, Roll 629 & 634.

————. *Register of Enlistments in the United States Army, 1798-1914, M233.* NARS, 1968, Rolls 25 & 26.

————. *Returns From Regular Army Cavalry Regiments, 1833-1916, M744.* NARS, Rolls 5 & 17.

————. *Returns From United States Military Posts, 1800-1916, M617.* NARS, 1968, Roll 285 & 595.

War of the Rebellion, Series I, Vol. L, Parts I & II.

Walla Walla (W.T.) *Washington Statesman.* 29 November 1861.

Webster's New Collegiate Dictionary. Springfield, MA: G. & C. Merriam, 1974.

1855 Wisconsin State Census.

200 Years In The Making. Ontario, OR: Malheur Publishing, 1976.

Index

References to Maps are in boldface.
References to Figures, Photos, and Drawings are in italics.